About the series

This series of books has been written for several groups of people
– those thinking of joining a union, or new members; those who
are just becoming active members; new and less experienced shop
stewards; and indeed anyone interested in trade unions today. It
aims to provide an introduction to the principles of basic trade
unionism by discussing a wide range of arguments and issues in
the five key areas covered by the books. In straightforward
language each book points the way towards the action that must
be taken by individual trade unionists and by the movement as a
whole if their goals are to be achieved.

About this book

This book deals with the why and the how of trade union
organization. It begins by explaining why, despite the many
complaints in the media, we still need them today. It moves on to
give practical advice about how unions work, how to win
recognition and how union members can build up their
organization and negotiate better agreements. But the book
doesn't just deal with union organization in the workplace.
National union policies, the role of the TUC, the need for links
with the Labour Party and the problems of organizing
unemployed members are also discussed.

Thanks to Jim Sutherland, Solihull
College of Technology, for his
helpful comments.

Getting Organized

Alan Campbell is Lecturer in Industrial Relations at the Institute of Extension Studies, University of Liverpool. He was formerly a Workers' Educational Association Trade Union Studies Tutor/ Organizer in Manchester.

John McIlroy is a former WEA Tutor in Trade Union Studies. He now teaches law and industrial relations in the Department of Extra-Mural Studies, University of Manchester.

Pan Trade Union Studies

Also available in this series

C. Aldred:
Women at Work

C. Baker and P. Caldwell:
Unions and Change Since 1945

P. Burns and M. Doyle:
Democracy at Work

D. Eva and R. Oswald:
Health and Safety at Work

Series editors

Peter Caldwell
Tutor/Organizer
Workers' Educational Association,
West Midlands

Alan Campbell
Lecturer in Industrial Relations
University of Liverpool

Mel Doyle
Assistant Secretary
Workers' Educational Association

Pan
Trade Union
Studies

Getting
Organized

Alan Campbell and
John McIlroy

Pan Original

Pan Books   London and Sydney

First published 1981 by Pan Books Ltd,
Cavaye Place, London SW10 9PG
© Alan Campbell, John McIlroy and the Workers'
Educational Association 1981
ISBN 0 330 26476 1
Phototypeset by Input Typesetting Ltd,
London SW19 8DR
Printed and bound in Great Britain by
Richard Clay (The Chaucer Press) Ltd,
Bungay, Suffolk

Contents

Introduction

Trade unions have never been more important. There has never been such a volume of public debate and argument, as to what their role and function should be. This book is intended for people who are thinking about joining, or have recently joined, a trade union and those who have recently become involved in union activity for the first time, perhaps as a shop steward or branch secretary. Its aim is to give you a better understanding of what trade unions are about and some basic guidance on what is involved in being an efficient and active union member or representative. Of course there is no substitute for practical experience, but hopefully some of the guidance, advice and practical hints you will come across in the following pages will help you to avoid some of the more fundamental pitfalls. We have tried to write in a simple, straightforward fashion and to take little for granted.

This book deals largely with the basic nuts and bolts of organizing and being active in a trade union. However, there has been increasing criticism of trade unions in recent years. Their activities are a constant preoccupation for politicians and a constant topic of conversation in the pub. The newspapers constantly assert that the progress made by trade unions has gone too far and should be reversed; that trade unions are running the country; that trade unions are no longer necessary to protect workers; that they do more harm than good.

In the first two chapters of this book, therefore, we look at why and how trade unions came into existence, what they do and why they are still important today. We then go on to look in the second chapter at some of the myths that dominate discussion about trade unions and the limited relationship that they bear to the reality of the situation. This is important because you cannot be an effective trade unionist unless you understand in your own mind what trade unions are about.

Having cleared some of the ground we then look at which unions organize which kinds of workers in which industries and some of the factors you may wish to take into account in deciding which union is going to be best for you. Many trade unionists participate at their place of work. They have no idea of the advantages and benefits to be gained by using the wider union bodies. One of the arguments in this book is that few workplace organizations in the 1980s with large scale unemployment and economic recession can go it alone. You need to know how your union operates outside the workplace and how it can help you. We look at this in Chapter four.

Despite progress in many fields, there is still no obligation on employers to recognize trade unions and bargain with them. Many employers still refuse to give workers this basic right. Chapter five, therefore, looks at the background of recognition disputes and some of the practical problems facing those trying to win recognition by their own endeavours. This, of course, is just a beginning and in Chapters six and seven we look at how you can go about developing strong workplace organization, what kind of agreement you will need and what rights and protection the law gives you. Many workers find all sorts of practical problems, things that they had just never thought about before, come up when they lose their virginity and take industrial action for the first time. Finally, in Chapter eight we look at how you can go about winning a strike if your employer drives you to this last resort.

Unfortunately it has not been possible to deal at length with the problems of women and coloured workers. The reader must look elsewhere for guidance on the specific organizing problems they face, although another book in this series, *Women at work* by Chris Aldred, contains a full discussion of the problems women face.

Our belief is that, warts and all, trade unions provide an opportunity for democratic participation for more people than any other organization in our society. Despite conflicts over purpose and policy the unions are a training ground for thousands in the values of democracy, solidarity, cooperation and internationalism. It is not surprising that the groups in today's society which attack these values attack the unions. Unions remain an essential protection for workers, an essential force for progress. If this book helps in some small way to create more union activists and more aware members, then it will have been successful.

Chapter One

Why do we need trade unions?

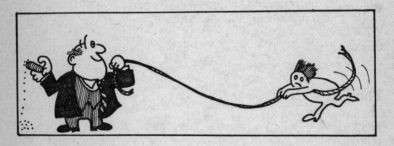

At your local on Friday night . . . on page two of the *Sun* . . . on your way to work . . . at half-time at the football match . . . at home when you switch on the television: you'll hear the same argument over and over and over. People argue that the advances made by trade unions over the past two hundred years have gone too far and should be reversed. They say, 'trade unions are running the country. That's not democratic.' They claim that union leaders don't represent their members. They even suggest sometimes that unions have outlived their usefulness, that they are no longer necessary.

Unless you are clear about *why* we have trade unions and are able to put the case for joining one, you're never going to get organized. So in this chapter we'll try to do the following things:

● show why and how trade unions developed;
● explain the basic principles on which they were built;
● demonstrate that these principles are still relevant today;
● put forward the arguments for joining a union.

We'll begin by looking at how unions were first organized in this country.

The Early Unions

'Gentlemen of the Jury. The charge imputed to the present defendants by the law of this country is a very heinous crime and is properly so considered, because the consequences of it must be very fatal to society; nothing can be more fatal to society, nothing can be more injurious to society than men meeting privately to do injury to large bodies of men, therefore, it has at all times been considered by the law of this country as a very serious offence. In the present instance, it not only affects the peace of society but also the commerce of the country and for that reason is punished by very severe penalties.'

This was the judge's summing up of the case against five printers who had organized a strike in 1798. In those days simply belonging to a trade union could result not only in dismissal; it could end in imprisonment. You could be arrested for attending a branch meeting. The next thing you knew you would be working as convict labour in Australia. Because of this, the early history of trade unionism is shrouded in mystery and secrecy. But looking at how the earliest unions came into existence helps us to understand why we have trade unions today.

In many towns in the eighteenth century there were trade clubs for the skilled members of each craft. They usually held their meetings in pubs and taverns. Sometimes the clubs would adopt the name of the tavern where they met, for example, the Globe Coachmakers. Sometimes the meeting place of a well-established society would take the name of the club. Pubs with names such as the Bricklayers Arms are a reminder of those early days.

The aims of these clubs were partly to provide sociable entertainment. After all, there was no television, football or bingo at that time. When apprentices had served their time, this was usually accompanied by much ceremony and drinking. There was no life insurance or social security benefits other than the shame and squalor of the workhouse. So the trade clubs were often also friendly and burial societies. In some trades they acted as a sort of 'labour exchange' where employers could contact and recruit skilled workers. (Union branches in the printing industry still carry on this function to the present day.)

One important job of the trade clubs was to ensure that craft customs and standards were maintained. They might insist on limiting the numbers of apprentices, depending on how many craftsmen there were. Given that the clubs provided a meeting place for workmen to discuss their trade it became a logical extension of their activity to fight for wage increases and to maintain their members' standards of living. This could often only be done effectively by linking up with other clubs in the same trade in the locality. A federation of trade clubs came to be known as a *trade union*.

Some craftsmen were self-employed. Others worked for small employers. But these employers sometimes looked on trade clubs indulgently. Many employers had themselves been skilled men who had saved enough money to set up in business employing a new journeyman. They often shared the attitudes of the craftsmen in maintaining the standards of the trade. Wages were often based on custom and practice rather than the law of supply and demand for labour. The pace of work was set according to the needs of the craftsman's skill. The craftsman therefore enjoyed considerable independence from his master in the workshop.

Many of the smallest employers would work side by side with their workmen. In such circumstances informal pressure could be exerted on the employer. Sometimes more formal sanctions had to be adopted by the trade club, such as advising members not to work for an employer whose wages were below the level set by the union. They had to be careful not to fall foul of the law, however. So long as *individuals* chose not to work for a particular employer that was legal. But if they were seen to combine collectively they were an illegal conspiracy. In 1799 and 1800 the Combination Acts were passed which made any trade union activity a crime punishable by three months' imprisonment. Although these acts were repealed in 1824, unions continued to suffer legal harassment throughout the nineteenth century.

The factory system

Apart from tradesmen working in small workshops in towns, the majority of the population during the eighteenth century worked on the land. But towards the end of the century, with the growth of mechanical means of production, there was a demand for labour in towns and villages. By and large, industry was still not organized on the basis of factories. Most machinery was so simple that it could be used in the workers' homes.

The work of the handloom weavers was typical of this 'domestic system' of cottage industry. Masters would deliver the yarn to the weavers and pay them for the finished cloth at the end of the week. The whole family would usually be employed, the father at the loom, younger children winding the thread on to bobbins, older children checking the cloth for faults, teenagers working a second or third loom, the wife also taking a turn as a break from housework. Like the craftsmen, the weavers also enjoyed a lot of independence in their work. If they drank too much over the week-end they could take Monday off and make up the lost time by working harder later in the week.

However, as more complicated, steam-driven machinery was invented, it was obviously impossible to operate it in people's houses. Instead, machines and workers were gathered together in factories and the system of work became

15

more intense. It's difficult for us today to understand just how great a change the spread of the factory system in the first half of the nineteenth century meant for workers and their families. In particular it meant:

- a growing social gap between employer and employed, because only the wealthiest masters could afford the cost of factories and machines;
- the disruption of the old, family-based system of work;
- the loss of the worker's independence in organizing his work;
- an almost total dependence on the pace of work set by machinery, often for long monotonous hours.

The following fictitious example illustrates how trade unions formed in response to these conditions.

John Ackerman, or 'Johnny Ackers' as he was known to his workmen, had been a small master employing fifteen spinners on a few machines. The process was fairly simple. The spinners' wives would clean the bales of raw cotton in their homes and their husbands would spin it into yarn in the workshop. The quality of their work was high. During the Napoleonic Wars with France, Ackerman had obtained highly profitable contracts to supply clothiers with thread to make soldiers' uniforms. These profits had been invested in building a large new factory employing 400 'hands'. Steam power was used to drive machines to clean the cotton so that the only work for the spinners' wives and children was winding and mending the yarn inside the factory itself.

Ackerman's mill produced cotton more cheaply and efficiently than the workshops of the smaller masters. As a result, he could undercut their prices and still make a profit. Many of the small masters had gone bust, their workmen had been taken on either by Ackerman or the other large mill owner in the town, Bernard Moneymaker.

Hours were long, often twelve or fourteen per day starting at five a.m. To make matters worse, the overlookers fiddled the works clock, putting it forward in the mornings and back at night. In this way, up to an extra half hour was cheated out of the workers. Although everyone knew this happened, no one was willing to speak out against the abuse for fear of the sack. Compared with the old workshops, conditions were dustier, hotter and noisier since there were many more machines and engines.

16

Wages were a constant source of grievance to the workers. When Tom Goodfellow, a married man with six children applied for work, Ackerman told him that the wages averaged 2s 10d per day for a good worker:

'I can't keep a family on that,' exclaimed Tom. 'Can't you make it three shillings?'

'I'm sorry but that is your problem, my good fellow,' explained Ackerman. 'There are five young men waiting at the gate willing to work at that rate. It's a free country, you can take it or leave it. But I'm a businessman, not a charitable institution.'

So take it Tom did, for what it was worth! But even with four of his six children at work amidst the mill's machines, the family could barely eke out a living. Wages were calculated on a payment by results system – according to the number of yards of thread the spinner produced from a given amount of cotton. The quality of the thread had to be approved by the overlooker. If it wasn't up to scratch then the rate for the job was reduced. Since the overlookers were always anxious to please Ackerman by outdoing each other in finding faults in the work, wages were often reduced.

The only legal redress for a workman cheated in this way was to summon his employer before a magistrate. Since the only two magistrates in Millsborough were John Ackerman and Bernard Moneymaker the chances of either winning a case, or of taking a case and keeping your job were slim.

If business was poor Ackerman simply laid his workers off for a month or two with no unemployment benefit or social security. They lived at near starvation. Discipline at Ackerman's mill was harsh. Any children who chanced to fall asleep during their long hours of labour would receive a beating with the overlooker's stick. Any spinner arriving a second after the starting hooter sounded would automatically lose a quarter of an hour's pay. Any questioning of the overlooker's authority could lead to the sack.

It was as a result of just such a case that a trade union first came to be formed at Ackerman's mill. A falling off in trade prompted Ackerman to reduce the spinners' rates of pay. The overlookers passed through the mill telling the men of the cut in wages. Just then a hot-headed young Irishman called Connell shouted out above the noise of the machines:

'Johnny Ackers is a blood-sucking leech on his poor workmen's necks!'

'Right,' said the overlooker, 'we'll have no truck with troublemakers like you in this mill. On your penny farthing, Paddy!'

In fact, by the standards of the time, Ackerman wasn't a particularly bad employer. He regularly made small payments to elderly ex-employees and those disabled by accidents in his mill. It genuinely distressed him to have to further reduce his men's pay. But he knew that Bernard Moneymaker, his arch-rival, had reduced his workers' wages the previous week. Unless he followed suit his prices would be undercut just as he had undercut so many of the smaller masters. He too might go bankrupt, so he had no choice but to follow Moneymaker's example.

That night, Connell's sacking and the cut in wages was the main topic of conversation around the tables in the Spinners Arms. As the men talked over their beer, Connell's temper got the better of him once more:

'Call yourselves men,' he snarled. 'You're no better than old women. We should be forming a union of spinners like they've done in Bolton and Bury. Unless we stand together and resist, Johnny Ackers'll drive our wages down beyond starvation level, which is where they are now!'

'That's just extremist talk, John,' said Tom Goodfellow. 'Some of us have families to think about. But perhaps if we were to get up a petition to Mr Ackerman he might change his mind.'

And so it was decided to draw up a petition which was duly signed by most of the men. It had no effect. Ackerman didn't even bother to reply and the wage cuts went ahead.

'It's been no damn good going begging to him on your hands and knees,' argued Connell in the Spinners Arms. 'He's cutting our wages because he can't afford not to. The only way to make him change his mind is to hit him where it counts, in his pocket. If we all stop work, his mill stops. If his mill stops there'll be no money coming in to pay off the bank for the new machinery he's put in. He can't afford to have that expensive machinery standing idle. If we're united it'll be cheaper for him in the long run to pay us the old rates. But he'll never do that unless Moneymaker pays his men the same. We'll have to persuade them that it's in all our interest for everyone to strike or it won't work.'

So the spinners of Millsborough set up a joint committee of delegates from Ackerman's and Moneymaker's to organize the strike and to link up with other committees in the surrounding towns. Meetings were held. Funds were collected from each man. The union was organized!

To sum up, Ackerman decided how much his workers were to be paid. He alone decided how hard or how long they would work. If he took a personal dislike to somebody he could deprive them of their livelihood. Ackerman was a one man dictator! No isolated individual could influence Ackerman's decisions. Only when there was collective organization could workers have any say at all in the important decisions that governed their lives. It was only when a trade union was introduced that the workers were able to question and challenge Ackerman's decisions. Only when the workers together voiced their views could Ackerman's factory be made more democratic.

The case described here is an imaginary one. But it isn't an unrealistic one. The rigorous control of the new factory masters can be seen by the list of fines, reproduced on page 20, imposed upon spinners at Tyldesley in 1823. The harsh conditions in one mill were described by a writer in the early nineteenth century:

'One poor boy was carrying an armful of bobbins from one flat to another. When ascending the stair he sat down to rest himself, as his legs were sore and swollen by incessant standing. In a few moments he was fast asleep. Whilst enjoying this stolen repose the master happened to pass. Without the least warning he gave him a violent slap on the head which stunned and stupefied him. In a half-sleeping state of stupefaction he ran to the moving frame, which he sometimes attended, and five minutes had barely elapsed when his left hand got entangled with machinery and two of his fingers were crushed to a jelly and had to be immediately amputated.'

It was against such conditions and low wages that Lancashire cotton spinners linked up in a loose federation of local societies called the 'Hercules' in 1818.

The principles of trade unionism

The above examples show the variety of ways in which workers' lives changed in the first half of the nineteenth century. The spread of factories and machinery was an uneven and drawn out process. It affected different groups of workers in different ways and at different times. But the

WORK – DISCIPLINE – FINES

A list of fines at Tyldesley

Any spinner found with his window open	1s
Any spinner found dirty at his work	1s
Any spinner found washing himself	1s
Any spinner leaving his oil-can out of its place	6d
Any spinner repairing his drum-banding, with his gas lighted	2s
Any piecer spilling water on the staircase, from a degging-can	1s
Any spinner slipping with his gas lighted	2s
Any spinner putting his gas out too soon	1s
Any spinner spinning with gaslight too long in the morning	2s
Any spinner having his lights too large, for each light.	1s
Any spinner heard whistling	1s
Any spinner having hard ends hanging on his weights	6d
Any spinner having hard ends on carriage-band	1s
Any spinner being five minutes after last bell rings	2s
Any spinner having roller laps, no more than two draws for each roller lap	6d
Any spinner going further than the roving room door, when fetching rovings	2s
Any spinner being sick, and cannot find another spinner to give satisfaction, must pay for steam, per day	6s
Any spinner found in another's wheel-gate	1s
Any spinner neglecting to send his sweepings three mornings in the week	1s
Any two spinners found together in the necessary, each man	1s
Any spinner having a little waste on his spindles	1s

SOURCE: *Cobbett's Political Register, August 1823.*

Note: The average weekly wage of a cotton spinner in the 1820s was little over £1.

basic principles on which they organized trade unions to defend their living standards were common to them all.

The conflict of interests between the employer and his workmen

Workers came to realize this most basic point as the old craft traditions were broken down. Before, the master craftsman's main desire was to demonstrate his skill in producing goods of the highest quality. This gave way to the industrialist's desire to produce goods as cheaply as possible in order to increase profits. This was not simply a case of individual greed. Unless the profits were used to invest in new plant and machinery he would be less efficient than other firms. He would be unable to compete with other manufacturers. His profits would decline and eventually he would go bankrupt.

From the employer's point of view, the same principles had to apply to his workers as to his machinery. They had to be employed as profitably as possible to keep costs down. In the harsh world of profit and loss accounts wages paid to workers were one more cost to be included in the same column as expenditure on raw materials or new equipment. Labour, like machinery, had to be bought as cheaply as possible. The higher the wages, the higher the costs. The higher the costs the lower the profits.

To the workers, wages were their only means of subsistence. If they fell to too low a level they would starve.

The conflict of interests between employer and workers was most obvious over the question of wages. However, it ran through every aspect of working life. 'Time is money' was nowhere more true than in the early factories. It was the employer's ideal to have his work-force productively employed for every second of the working day. And the longer they worked the better. Five minutes spent smoking in the toilet was five minutes not spent working. So a system of close supervision, fines for 'idleness', the constant threat of dismissal and even physical violence were used to keep workers working. Piece-work systems based on payment by

21

output were introduced so that the workers drove themselves to work harder.

Bargaining strength

Employers didn't have it all their own way, however, as we've seen. As more and more workers became involved in industry they became aware that their interests were often at odds with those of their boss. The problem was, what to do about it?

In theory, each individual worker was a free agent, able to enter into a contract of employment with the employer. The worker offered himself for hire. He was willing to work under the employer's direction for a set period. In return, the employer was willing to pay him wages for the work done. In theory, these were the two equal sides of the 'wages for labour' relationship.

In practice, the worker had little choice but to sell his labour at whatever wage the employer was willing to pay. It's true that if he didn't like the rate being offered for the job he was free to take his services elsewhere, but the pressure of competition forced all employers to set wages as low as possible and if the worker exercised his freedom not to work for any of them he couldn't survive.

In this market for labour, not all workers were equal. Those with skills could expect to be paid more than unskilled labourers because their skills and knowledge of a particular job were in short supply. Since there were plenty of unskilled workers with nothing to offer but their physical strength their wages were lower. If you had no skills and weren't physically strong then you were at the bottom of the heap.

The craftsmen sought to preserve this privileged position by uniting the numbers of men who became skilled. This was done by the apprenticeship system. Only those willing to undergo training at lower wages for up to seven years would qualify for craftsmen's wages. The limited availability of their skills gave them a potential power over their employer. They were in a strong bargaining position because they couldn't easily be replaced. If they decided to withdraw their labour, the employer would be unable to operate the factory and would lose money. It might therefore be cheaper to meet the workers' demands.

But even the skilled craftsman was in an unequal bargaining position with his employer if other workers with similar skills were willing to work for lower wages or under worse conditions. The trade clubs and unions soon learned that they could only hope to exert pressure on their employer if they did it collectively. Only by acting together could workers gain any real bargaining power.

'Unity is strength'

This is probably one of the oldest trade union slogans. Only by combining together could groups of workers ensure that union rules were uniformly observed. Only by combining together to withdraw their labour could they increase wages. Only by combining together could they protect individuals from being picked on or sacked. As the old trade unionists used to say, 'Pick up a match and try to break it . . . it's easy. Now pick up twenty matches and try to break them . . . that's what trade unions are all about!'

The development of trade unions

It's easy to speak about unity. In practice, the task of building a united movement among different groups of workers was a hard, uphill struggle which demanded great discipline and sacrifice. One well-used definition of a trade union is:

> '. . . a continuous association of wage earners for the purpose of maintaining and improving the condition of their working lives.'

However, there were many barriers to establishing continuous trade union organization. This was particularly true of unskilled workers. Throughout the nineteenth century most union members were in the skilled trades. Only a minority of the total working population were in unions. Unskilled jobs were often done by floating, casual labourers who were often affected by spells of unemployment. It was extremely difficult to organize this kind of worker into permanent unions. If they did manage to combine together and go on strike, it was easier for the employer to replace them with non-union strike-breakers than it was with skilled workers.

Even among skilled workers, organization was never easy. Before the second half of the nineteenth century almost all unions were locally based. They didn't have the resources of today's national unions. They were often short of funds to support their striking members and if a strike was defeated the union often simply collapsed. On occasions the responsibility for looking after the funds proved too great a temptation for some branch treasurers and they skipped town with the members' cash! The need for a self-disciplined approach to union organization is indicated in the rule books of some of the early unions. The Articles of the Society of Journeymen Brushmakers rule that:

'. . . there shall be a president chosen from the members present to keep order . . . If any member dispute on politics, swear, lay wagers, promote gambling or otherwise behave disorderly, and will not be silent when ordered by the chairman he shall pay a fine of one shilling.'

From these early attempts at formal organization the modern British trade union movement developed. There is no space to describe the history of the movement here. However, the figures on trade union membership shown in Figure 1 chart the pattern of union growth.

The graph shows a steady growth in membership between 1892 and 1920 – from just over one and a half million to almost five and a half million. Much of this expansion was due to growing organization among unskilled groups such as dockers and transport workers. The 1890s and 1900s were marked by many strikes in which the unskilled fought to organize unions and force their employers to negotiate with them.

This trend continued during the years of the First World War. To secure union support for the war effort the govern-

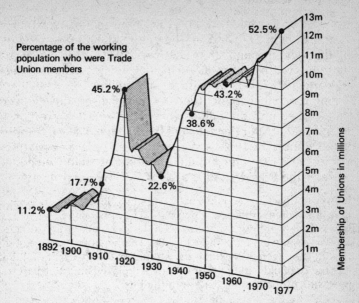

Figure 1. Trade union membership in Britain: 1892–1977

ment allowed union membership to grow in the vast munitions industry. Moreover, the shortage of manpower during the war increased workers' bargaining power to win union recognition from employers.

By 1920, the trade union movement covered nearly half of the working population. Trade unions were stronger than ever before. Then disaster struck.

The years after the war saw a sharp fall in union membership. It was almost halved between 1920 and 1933. The reason for this was the mass unemployment in the depression years of the 1920s and '30s. By 1933 there were three million unemployed, 23 per cent of the total working population. Because millions of workers who had previously been in a union were out of work, they left the union. For those who were lucky enough to have jobs, being a trade unionist was much more difficult. Because there were more people than there were available jobs, the bargaining power of the employers was greatly increased. It was harder for unions to

25

negotiate improved terms and conditions, so many members became demoralized and left the union. The number of working days lost through strikes between 1933 and 1939 was just over one and a half million. In the militant years between 1919 and 1921 it was over forty-nine million.

Union members who tried to organize effectively were often sacked and the unions were in too weak a position to defend them. After the defeat of the General Strike in support of the miners in 1926, some employers only allowed their workers to return on condition they left the union. Abe Moffat, later the President of the Scottish Miners, recalled:

'I never got back in the Fife Coal Company. Never. Never. I eventually got a job in a pit way down in Clackmannanshire. A small pit it was. They were not connected with the Coal-owners' Association so I was able to get a job there in 1938. That went for the rest of my family. They were all victimized. My father too. It was general all over the coalfield. All the people who had played an active part had great difficulty in getting back into the pits.'

With the return of full employment during the Second World War and the post-war years, the number of union members gradually increased once more. Union membership began to decline in the 1960s, but since 1968 there has been a steady increase. In 1974, union 'density' topped the 50 per cent mark. For the first time in British history more than half of the working population were trade union members. In fact, the work-force in Britain is one of the best organized in the world. In the United States, for example, there were twenty-three million union members, only 20 per cent of the work-force. In France, also, the figure is about 20 per cent.

The development of union objectives

As we've seen, unions developed in this country to fight for better wages and conditions – for a better standard of living for working people. Although improving wages is often thought of as the main aim of unions, it's not the only one. The range of objectives which the trade union movement has set itself in recent years has been summarized by the TUC as follows:

improved terms of employment;
improved physical environment at work;
full employment and national prosperity;
security of employment and income;
improved social security;
fair shares in national income and wealth;
industrial democracy;
a voice in government;
improved public and social services;
public control and planning of industry.

The first two objectives relate directly to working conditions. They mean not just improved wages but shorter working hours and longer holiday. Union concern with the 'physical environment at work' is reflected in the large number of recently appointed union safety representatives whose job it is to look after health and safety at work.

However, union objectives are not just about what goes on in the workplace. Today, many factors outside the workplace can affect the living standards of union members.

For example:
● The level of tax will influence how much pay actually ends up in the worker's pocket.
● Government incomes policies may restrict a trade union's ability to negotiate freely on wages.
● Welfare benefits will determine income levels of workers and their families when they are sick, or unemployed, or old.
● The level of unemployment influences how easy it is for workers to find jobs. Trade unions have argued that to produce full employment there has to be greater public control and planning of how industry is run.
● Laws which limit the ability of unions to organize effectively such as the 1971 Industrial Relations Act or the 1980 Employment Act.
● The standards of the education system and the National

Health Service will affect the general quality of life of workers and their families.

So trade union action in the workplace isn't, by itself, sufficient to guarantee an improved standard of living. In many cases, unions have to exert political as well as industrial pressure. We'll look at this question of 'unions and politics' in more detail in the next chapter, but we can see already that the aims of trade unions have been extended since the days of the early combinations and trade clubs. However, the basic principles on which trade unions were built remain the same.

Some people agree that trade unions were necessary 'in the bad old days'. But they argue that living standards have risen greatly in the last hundred years – so there's no longer a need for trade unions. Let's look at this argument by first considering the following fictitious example, then reconsidering the basic principles of trade unionism.

Before 1975 the clerical staff at the family firm of Superior Products Ltd had seen little need for joining a trade union. Indeed, many were hostile to the very idea. 'Unions might be necessary for the shop-floor', they would argue, 'but we're all right because we've got staff status.' This meant that they were better paid, and on a salaried basis. They didn't have to clock in and out of work and they didn't lose any money if they were a few minutes late. They had longer holidays than the manual workers as well as good sick pay and pension schemes. There were also the additional perks of the staff canteen, staff toilets, and a general easy-going atmosphere in the offices. Relations between individual employees and the various directors were good and sometimes on first name terms. Insofar as the staff employees were organized collectively, it was through the Superior Staff Association. This body was subsidized by the company. Its main function was to organize the Christmas social and pensioners' outings, although the secretary sat on the company consultative committee.

But not everything in the garden was rosy. The first rumblings of discontent were over pay. There were what management called 'individual assessments' each year to decide on each employee's incremental increase and bonus payment. As Al Smith said, 'It's bloody unfair, it's just Bill Jones who decides how much we're to get . . .' 'You're dead right,' everyone agreed, 'but what can you do about it?'

Because some employees had relatives who worked on the shop-floor, the staff were aware of the decreasing differential between their salaries and the actual earnings of the manual workers who had recently signed a favourable productivity deal. People grumbled, but there wasn't much they could do as individuals. The staff association was consulted about changes in the general pay scales, but it took no part in the individual assessments. The erosion was further emphasized when the shop-floor workers' union began negotiations on sickness and pension schemes. 'Before we know where we are, they'll be better off than us,' complained Al Smith.

The next change was the takeover of the firm by a multinational company. The first thing the staff knew about the deal was when they were told about it by the shop-floor union convenor. The old directors were soon replaced by a new management team which began a 'rationalization' programme. The old free and easy atmosphere changed. People who left weren't replaced and the pace of work intensified. The last straw was the proposed introduction of a computerization scheme to handle stock control and invoicing, to be accompanied by a staff training programme. Management announced that there would have to be 20 per cent redundancies among the staff.

The staff ran round like headless chickens. The secretary of the staff association felt that they ought to accept the situation out of loyalty to the firm: 'Look at all the advantages the company has given us in the past.' But some of the other employees were unconvinced: 'How much have they had out of me in the last twenty years?' 'What's the good of staff status if some of us don't have a job?' They began to talk about the need for a union: 'The shop-floor workers wouldn't let themselves be treated like this . . .'

For several weeks the arguments raged on. In the end, several of them joined APEX, the clerical workers' union. The word went round, interest grew and a lunchtime meeting of staff was held in a nearby pub. After a lot of discussion, the local union official said, 'It's the same everywhere, new technology leads to redundancies and job changes . . . if you want protection you've got to join a union.' In the end, most of those present joined up. A branch was set up and a committee elected. Soon more than three-quarters of the staff were union members.

The company was far from happy about these developments. However, the union won its first victory when the shop-steward insisted on being present during members' individual assessments and, by comparing various cases, managed to win increases for a number of staff. The balance of forces was now tilting in favour of the new union. The branch threatened to refuse to operate the new computer unless negotiations took place. It threatened industrial action if any union member was made redundant. The shop-floor union, also fearful of redundancy, offered its support. The union officials consulted with ACAS, the Advisory, Conciliation and Arbitration Service, and it advised the company to fully recognize the union. At last the company gave in and agreed to negotiate. In the end, no jobs were lost.

So is there still a conflict of interest between employers and workpeople? We'd argue that there is. We'd agree that working conditions today are very different from those of the industrial revolution. We might be able to put a man on the moon, we may even be able to guarantee him a soft landing, but the question remains – how much are we going to pay him? The staff employees described above enjoyed a far higher standard of living than the workers in Ackerman's cotton mill. They may have had a decent canteen and pleasant offices. They may have got some help from ACAS. But their relationship with their employer was fundamentally the same as that between Ackerman and his hired hands. Their interests were not the same as those of the multinational company. As isolated individuals they were powerless midgets against a huge giant. They could exert no control over the decisions affecting their working lives. Only by acting collectively could they bring pressure to bear.

Even today, the average worker can only live by selling his ability to work to an employer. The worker depends on the price of that labour to exist. The employer buys it because he thinks he can sell the product of the worker's labour for more than he has paid the worker to make it. The difference between what he pays the worker and what he sells the product at is the source of his profit. Therefore the cheaper the worker's wages the higher the employer's profits.

The other problem is, of course, how the labour is used once the employer has bought it – in other words, how hard and in what conditions you will work once you are taken on.

A fair day's work for a fair day's pay. The problem is that the employer's ideas of fairness tend to be very different from the worker's. It was true in Ackerman's day and it's true today. There is still a constant conflict at work because of this. Dempsey versus Tunney . . . Ali versus Frazier . . . Leonard versus Duran. Over time the personalities change but the fight goes on. Whether it's Britain, South Africa, . . . or even Poland, wherever there's a 'wages for labour' relationship, workers will always insist on joining trade unions.

It's often said in the press and television that if only employers and workers would stop being at loggerheads and work as a team then everyone would be more prosperous. Workers and employers, some people argue, have a common interest in the enterprise producing a surplus of wealth. But the heart of the problem is this: the conflict then arises over how that surplus is divided between shareholders' profits, investment in research, plant and machinery and increased wages for the workers.

Whether we like it or not, the laws of the market-place apply just as much today as they did in Ackerman's mill. If employers can't produce competitively they go bust. There is still a constant pressure on them to reduce wages and increase profits.

Only the collective power of trade union organization can provide a counter-pressure to maintain living standards. It's notable that in the industries where unions are weakest, wages are lowest. It's true that wages can sometimes be relatively high in some non-unionized companies. But this is usually only because unions exist in other companies producing similar goods. If the non-union company wants to attract good workers, then it has to pay the going rate for the job negotiated by the unions in the other companies. So what is happening is that the unions are indirectly influencing wages in the non-union company.

When unions are weakly organized throughout an entire industry – for example, the catering industry – then wages are held down throughout the industry. If we look abroad, to countries where no trade unions exist at all, wages and conditions are just as bad as they were in Britain during the industrial revolution. A recent report on child labour in South America described children employed underground in coal mines. They work pulling wagons of coal along narrow underground passages, just as they did in Britain in the 1830s.

The interests of employers and workers still diverge and often conflict. Trade unions don't create this conflict. It's built into the way work is organized. However, today, because of the existence of trade unions, it's possible to resolve these conflicts through *collective bargaining*. This means that representatives of the union and the employer sit down to bargain and negotiate. Because there is a conflict of interests, each side will have its own aims as to what it wants out of the negotiations. The outcome of this bargaining is a collective agreement. What is important about the process of collective bargaining is that it gives workers a say in the decisions that affect their working lives.

For example, if management in a workplace which is organized want to introduce new machinery or methods of working, this will have to be negotiated with the unions. The unions will want to ensure that jobs will not be lost and that their members are paid more if the machinery demands new skills. The proposed changes won't take place until management and unions have reached an agreement on these issues. Compare the situation the Luddites faced 150 years ago. Because trade unions were illegal then, the workers couldn't protect themselves by negotiation – the only alternative was rioting and machine-breaking. Today such disputes can be settled by collective bargaining.

Similarly, in the days when union organization was weak or non-existent, workers had no right of redress against management discipline. If your face didn't fit, you could be sacked on the spot. Today, there are clear disciplinary procedures for unions to defend their members.

Usually neither side gets its own way completely in such negotiations. Agreements can often only be reached by compromise from each party. But both sides agree to abide by the terms of the agreement.

Just how favourable the outcome of collective bargaining

is to either side will be determined by the bargaining strength of management and unions at the time the negotiations take place. If the balance of forces favours management – such as a high level of unemployment – the union may be forced to accept an agreement well short of its original aim. We'll look more closely at how agreements are negotiated in a later chapter.

We can now summarize the main points about why you should join a union:

- Employers and employees have different interests which often conflict.
- A trade union is a democratic association of working people formed to protect their interests.
- Unions enable you and your workmates to speak with one voice and win through collective bargaining what can't be gained through individual negotiation.
- Trade unions seek to improve their members' wages and conditions, but that's not all they do. The union will defend you if you face disciplinary action from your employer. It will try and make sure that your job is safe from redundancy. If you are injured at work the union will provide legal advice about claiming compensation you may be entitled to.
- Being in a trade union gives you a say in your own future and the future of your industry.

However, even if people accept that trade unions *are* still necessary, many are critical of the way that they operate. In the next chapter we'll consider some of the most common complaints.

Further reading

T. Lane, *The Union Makes Us Strong* (Arrow, 1974) is a readable introduction to the history of trade unions in this country. C. Baker and P. Caldwell, *Unions and Change Since 1945* (Pan, 1981) discusses the changing nature of trade union membership. Several of the essays in *The Incompatibles*, edited by R. Blackburn and A. Cockburn (Penguin, 1967) discuss the basic principles of trade unionism and their role in today's society, as does V. Allen's *Militant Trade Unionism* (Merlin, 1966). You may find some of the ideas complex at first, but they repay study.

Chapter Two

Arguments about unions

There has been increasing criticism of trade unions in recent years, much of it ill-informed. You can hardly open a newspaper or switch on television without reading or hearing about 'the trade union problem'. Unions are blamed for everything from the high cost of living to bubonic plague. If you want to be an effective trade unionist, you need to able to take up the arguments in favour of trade unions. You have to discuss the issues convincingly with your workmates when they start quoting the latest 'trade union atrocity story'

from the *Sun* or the *Express*. So in this chapter we'll consider the following issues:

● Are the unions too powerful?
● Are unions undemocratic?
● Is the closed shop a threat to individual freedom?
● Are strikes the cause of Britain's economic problems?
● Do high wages cause inflation and unemployment?
● Does the country need cuts in public expenditure because of unproductive workers?
● Are unions too political?

Trade unions have too much bargaining power

A common theme in current discussion of trade unions is that they are far too powerful. Trade union leaders are described as being like 'mediaeval robber barons', extorting far more than a fair share for their members out of the poor and needy industrialist. Some people have gone so far as to suggest, particularly during the period of the Labour government from 1974–9, that the trade unions 'were running the country'.

Now it's true that industry, and indeed society in general, has grown more complicated. This means that when collective bargaining breaks down and a group of workers decides to go on strike to bring pressure to bear on their employer, the effects are often far reaching. However, as the 1968 Royal Commission on Trade Unions indicated, striking is an unusual activity for most workers.

Those people who suggest that trade unions use the strike weapon too frequently should remember that strikes only occur when workers withdraw their labour. They therefore appear to be the villains when, in fact, they are often reacting to an arbitrary decision by management. Surely if trade unions had the power they are alleged to have, they would not need to lose money to resolve a problem. They would simply inform management of the required solution and management would have to implement it.

To suggest that unions have more power than employers

just doesn't make sense to most union members. Yet it's widely believed. To realize just how unrealistic a proposition it is, ask yourself when was the last time you read about a shop-steward sacking the managing director?

In fact, it is employers who are getting more powerful. An ongoing process of mergers and takeovers means that more and more economic power is concentrated among fewer companies. In 1909, the hundred largest manufacturing companies accounted for only 16 per cent of the net output of manufacturing industry in Britain. By 1970, the share of the top hundred companies had risen to 41 per cent. In 1976–7, the combined assets of the twenty largest companies in the UK amounted to almost £30.5 billion. Between them they employed 1,266,237 workers in Britain. They controlled about 8000 subsidiary companies throughout the world. This means that these companies possess huge resources. The decisions they make on the use and allocation of these resources can affect the lives of everyone in Britain as consumers, and in some cases employees. It is precisely this sort of power which trade unions today do *not* have.

When trade unions exercise what power they do have, it is usually in response to something which employers have done – such as sacking the shop-steward! Unions are primarily defensive organizations. They have little power to initiate change. It's sometimes stated that one 'acid test' of power in society is how much influence a social group can exert on the distribution of economic resources. On this score, unions haven't advanced since 1900. From that date there hasn't been any significant change in the way national income is divided up. Recent reports of the Royal Commission on the Distribution of Wealth and Income show just how much wealth the 'top people' own. See Figure 2.

As to the specific question of whether the trade unions 'are running the country', it's true that the trade union movement is often consulted by the government of the day. After all, more than half of the working population are in trade unions. But this doesn't mean that the government always, or even often, takes the TUC's advice. For example, the trade unions have been campaigning for a number of years, largely un-

In 1974 ... How the 'wealth cake' was divided:

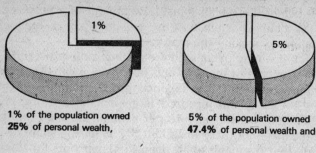

1% of the population owned
25% of personal wealth,

5% of the population owned
47.4% of personal wealth and

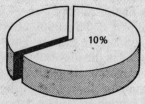

10% of the population owned
61.5% of personal wealth

Figure 2. How personal wealth was shared among the population in 1974

Source: Royal Commission on the Distribution of Income and Wealth.

successfully, for the government to adopt their 'alternative economic strategy' to combat unemployment.

It's also true that in recent years, the power of Parliament as the highest governing body has been eroded. But that power has not ebbed away into the hands of the trade union movement. Rather, the economic powers of the financial institutions and multinational corporations have proved stronger than national parliaments. As yet, trade unionists have no seats on the boards of these institutions or any say in the economic and industrial policies they pursue. And if we look at who administers power in this country – the top civil servants, the high court judges, the senior police officers – trade unionists are again conspicuous by their absence.

Given the size and potential power of trade unions what is perhaps most surprising is not that 'they're running the country' (because they're not!), but how little impact they've had in redistributing wealth and power in our society.

Unions are undemocratic

Not only do trade unions have too much power, goes the popular myth, but they exercise that power undemocratically. In its evidence to the Royal Commission on Trade Unions, the TUC argued the opposite position. The very essence of trade unionism was its democratic principles.

What do we mean when we speak about 'trade union democracy?' We'd suggest there are two crucial dimensions.

First, it means that the policies adopted by trade unions should reflect the views of the majority of the membership. In most trade union rule books, there is provision for the members in their branches to discuss issues and formulate proposals to be sent for discussion at the union's national conference. The conference is attended by delegates, who are either elected directly by the members in the branches, or sometimes indirectly by other elected divisional and regional committees. So unions do have the machinery for reaching decisions democratically.

However, one general problem is that branches are often poorly attended in some unions. This can mean that the few members who attend branch meetings may be unrepresentative of the membership as a whole. This problem is common to all voluntary organizations, whether it's the local darts club or a trade union. We'll look at some of the reasons why members don't show up at union meetings and how you can try and improve attendance in a later chapter.

The second aspect of union democracy is that the people who carry out union policies should be accountable to the membership for their actions. The most readily accessible union official in the workplace is the shop-steward. He comes up for regular re-election. He's directly accountable to the members in the factory or office for the way he implements union policy. If they don't like him they can get rid of him. With regard to full-time officials, some are elected, many are appointed. Their members don't therefore have a direct influence on them. But they're usually appointed by, and answerable to, the union-elected executive committee. Similar points can be made about general secretaries. Some are appointed, many are elected, albeit for life. Nevertheless, formally at least, they are responsible to an elected executive.

To sum up, unions are run on democratic principles. This is not to deny that some have more democratic features than others. And no union member would claim that his organization was perfect. But all unions share the general principles of democratic policy making, elected delegate committees and officials who are directly or indirectly accountable to the members. If members feel there are shortcomings in the way their unions are run, then democratic channels exist to change them. But this can only happen if they fully and actively participate in their branches and workplaces. If they don't, then they can't justifiably complain that the union isn't representing them.

What is remarkable about trade unions is not that they are undemocratic (though some may have undemocratic features). In general they constitute one of the few powerful institutions in contemporary society which are organized on a democratic basis. If we turn once more to the twenty largest companies in the United Kingdom, we find that their enormous wealth and power rests in the hands of just 288 men who sit on their governing boards. Their one and a quarter million employees have no say either in their appointment or the policies they pursue. If we look at the popular press, which is so fond of pointing to the alleged defects in the trade union movement, there is a conspicuous absence of any democratic control. After all, no one 'elected' Rupert Murdoch to be the owner of the *Sun*, the *News of the World* and *The Times*!

The closed shop is a threat to individual freedom

What is a closed shop? It means either prospective employees must be union members before they are taken on (a pre-entry closed shop) or, much more commonly, they are given a period in which they have to join a union *after* they are hired (a post-entry closed shop).

Why do trade unionists need the closed shop? The basis of trade unionism is that we gain more by acting together than by acting separately. Employees as individuals can exert little control over their lives at work. Without the collective support of fellow workers they are exposed to the arbitrary power of the employer. The more employees there are in the union, the stronger that union is. As the TUC stated in its evidence to the Royal Commission on Trade Unions:

'The logical objective of a trade union in terms of organization is clearly 100 per cent organization; in other words, to bring about a situation in which all workers in the relevant trade belong to the union . . .'

Complaints are often heard from the media and Conservative Party politicians that trade unions which enforce 100 per cent organization are unjustifiably 'limiting individual freedom'. However, when you think about it, restrictions on individual liberties for the common good are widespread. For example, we all have to pay taxes, drive on the left-hand side of the road and stop at red traffic lights. We don't have the individual choice of opting out. If you believe that trade unions are essential to defend working conditions and living standards and to give workers some say in how their workplace is run, then the stronger the union is, the more likely that these aims will be achieved. Some individual restrictions are acceptable to reach these collective goals.

In practice, individuals *don't* negotiate their own terms and conditions of employment. These are negotiated collectively by trade union officials, supported in terms of time and money by their members. The non-unionists take all the benefits won for them by others without contributing a penny themselves or taking any personal risks. This is indirectly the case even in workplaces where there is no trade union organization at all. (See page 31). The closed shop prevents the unfairness of such 'free-riding'.

Some trade unionists may say: 'Shouldn't we negotiate certain standards for union members only'? You may use this as an argument to convince a worker to join a union, but if we put this into practice it would mean that we would have a group of poorly-paid workers outside union discipline, subject to management manipulation and representing an argument for low wages for everyone else.

Sometimes the opponents of the closed shop invoke the 'right' *not* to belong to a trade union as being equally valid as the right to belong to one. However, as most employers will not negotiate with individuals, this so-called right not to belong simply undermines the bargaining position of fellow workers and allows everyone's conditions to deteriorate. The closed shop attempts to stop such people from hurting their workmates and ultimately themselves. Against this negative 'right' not to belong to a union, trade unionists can equally legitimately claim a right not to have to work alongside non-union free-riders.

A further argument sometimes used against the closed shop is that workers may lose their job if they happen to lose their union card through an unreasonable decision by the union to expel them. Despite the fact that the people who most frequently use this argument rarely shed any tears when workers lose their jobs through the unreasonable actions of employers, their case needs to be taken seriously. The argument has both strengths and weaknesses. Yes – unions aren't perfect and cases have occurred when some members appear to have been unreasonably deprived of membership; but such cases are few and far between, a handful exaggerated out of all proportion to the total number of members covered by closed shop agreements.

However, even a few are too many. We have to press constantly for the fullest democracy within unions and the strictest safeguards for all members. To this end, the TUC set up an Independent Review Committee in 1976 which consists of an academic industrial relations expert, a distinguished lawyer and a retired union general secretary. It hears appeals from people who have been sacked as a result of being expelled from a union where there is a closed shop. The committee investigates the case and can either recommend that the member be reinstated or else upholds the union's decision. In this way, any potential abuses of the closed shop can be prevented.

Strikes are the cause of Britain's economic problems

First, let's put the so called 'strike problem' into perspective. We've already noted that, for the average worker, strikes are a very uncommon occurrence. As the Department of Employment stated in 1978:

'Strikes in industry are generally confined to a few sectors of industry while the vast majority of industry is strike free.'

Nor is Britain particularly strike-prone in comparison with other countries. The International Labour Office recently published figures which show how Britain rates in the international league table of working days lost through industrial disputes between 1967 and 1976. These are shown in Figure 3. This shows the annual average number of days lost per 1000 people in the mining, manufacturing, construction and transport industries. Seven countries lost a higher number of days than Britain. These included Finland, Australia, the United States, Italy and Canada. But this, of course is not the main point. Workers in these countries, with the possible exception of Italy, are better off than we are. Perhaps there is a lesson there for trade unionists!

In addition, the number of days lost through sickness and industrial injury is far greater than the number lost through strikes. For example, in 1977 under ten million working days were lost through disputes. 300 million were lost through sickness and about twenty million from industrial injury. Yet no one suggests that industrial injuries are the cause of Britain's economic problems!

Why then are strikes often seen as a major threat to society? In part it's because strikes do pose a threat to managerial authority and control in the workplace. By applying the strike sanction, trade unions can often pressurize management into yielding a greater say on wages and working conditions.

In part it's because strikes are usually treated in a sensational way by the media. If an editor has the choice between

43

the following stories, which one do you think he will run as his headline:

10 WORKERS GO DEAF AS A RESULT OF NOISY MACHINERY

or

10 MEN STRIKE OVER SHOP STEWARD SACKED
FOR MAKING LOVE
TO MANAGING DIRECTOR'S WIFE.

Television and the majority of newspapers take a hostile position towards trade unions. Most editors share managerial views and attitudes. As a result, both the TUC and independent researchers have criticized the bias in their coverage of trade union affairs. This often makes workers feel defensive but in fact strikes are natural in our society.

Can strikes be avoided? No. Although trade unions and employers attempt to resolve their conflicts through the process of collective bargaining, sometimes they fail to reach a mutually acceptable agreement. If we accept that workers are collectively free to sell their labour, we must also accept that they are collectively free not to sell their labour. They will go on strike until the employer agrees to their terms. Alternatively, if his bargaining strength is greater, the employer may lock-out his employees, refuse to buy their labour, until they agree to his terms. Given the conflict of interest at the centre of industrial relations, some strikes are going to be inevitable. Ultimately, workers have no other means to defend themselves against management decisions they disagree with, except by walking out. If you can't go on strike the employer can make you do anything he wants.

Wages cause inflation

One of the most persistent topics in current discussion on trade unionism is the argument that high wage settlements are the main cause of inflation – the rising cost of living. 'If only trade unionists would stop asking for higher wages then the cost of living would stop going up.' This assertion is repeated so often that it is unhesitatingly accepted as a basic

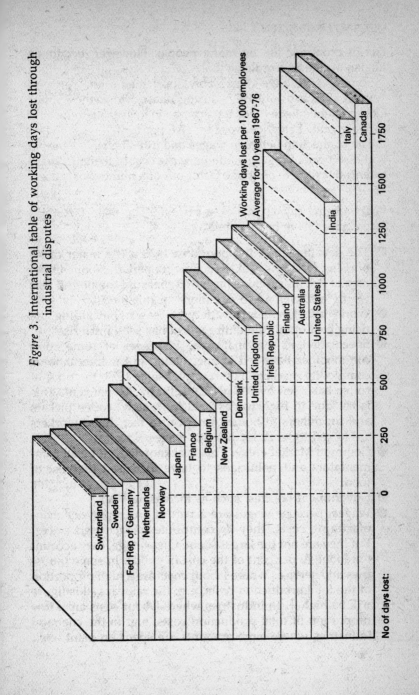

Figure 3. International table of working days lost through industrial disputes

Working days lost per 1,000 employees
Average for 10 years 1967-76

No of days lost:

Switzerland
Sweden
Fed Rep of Germany
Netherlands
Norway
Japan
France
Belgium
New Zealand
Denmark
United Kingdom
Irish Republic
Finland
Australia
United States
India
Italy
Canada

0   250   500   750   1000   1250   1500   1750

fact of economic life by many people. However, economic life isn't quite as simple as that.

Some people have remarkably short memories. Between August 1976 and July 1977, during phase two of the Labour Government's Social Contract, wage increases were limited to 5 per cent. Yet prices rose by 17.6 per cent.

The connection between wages and inflation isn't a simple and direct one. Wages *do* influence the cost of living to some extent. But they're only one factor out of a number of causes.

What are the causes of rising prices? The main factors in recent years have been as follows.

- The devaluation of the pound in 1976 was a major cause of rising food prices in the following period. About 45 per cent of Britain's food is imported. Because the pound was worth less, we had to pay more for this food.
- World inflation. For a variety of reasons, including the rising cost of oil, the entire world has seen price rises.
- Speculation in raw materials. Shortages of some basic commodities have led to speculation in the international commodity markets. For example, since 1973, the price of coffee has risen by 900 per cent, tin by 300 per cent. This is *not* due to high wages paid to 'greedy' coffee pickers and tin miners in South America. In fact, these workers are forced to work for poverty wages.
- Common Market entry. This is acknowledged by all commentators and politicians to have increased the cost of food.
- Government policies, such as increasing VAT.
- Wages. Because wages are a part of an employer's manufacturing costs, they *do* contribute to increased prices. But they are not the largest item. On average, they account for about 40 per cent of the cost of goods. In some industries and services where labour costs are a high proportion of the total production costs, e.g. the railways, this figure will be higher. In industries where labour costs are a low proportion of total production costs, e.g. in the chemical industries where large amounts are spent on plant, etc.,

wages have much less influence on price. Wage costs are lowest in some of the areas with the highest increases. No one claims that food prices are high because of farm labourers wages, or that house prices are high because of building workers' wages.

So if people try and say that inflation is *all* down to the trade unions they're wrong. Because wage costs only average 40 per cent of total costs, a 20 per cent wage increase means only an extra 8 per cent in total costs. Yet in many instances, employers use a wage increase to justify a price increase of the same size – a 20 per cent price increase being blamed on a 20 per cent wage increase.

The problem of inflation can't be solved simply by workers not getting pay increases. If workers didn't get *any* wage increases, prices would still go up, though not by quite as much – workers of course would starve! Trade unionists have little choice but to attempt to maintain living standards by seeking wage increases in line with the cost of living. What's 'greedy' about that? The problem of inflation will only be solved when the government takes action to control price increases. Workers are not responsible for running the economy. Why should they be responsible for the problems of that economy? If society, as it is organized today, can't provide workers with a living wage, then perhaps workers will have to change society.

But not only do higher wages lead to higher inflation, goes the argument, they also lead to higher unemployment. Workers are said to be 'pricing themselves out of a job' because if wage costs are too high then a) the overall costs of products and services will rise and employers won't be able to sell them, and b) employers will have less money for investment and so enterprises will become less competitive. In reality, things are more complicated.

Between the summer of 1974 and 1979, the average take home pay in *real* terms, i.e. once price increases are taken into account, did not increase. Indeed, between 1975 and 1977 the value of real wages fell. Yet throughout this period the trend of unemployment was upwards. Indeed, some of the most swingeing job losses have taken place in industries whose wage rates are well *below* the average, for example textiles and clothing.

Since 1979, the increase in unemployment has been dramatic. In 1980, John Biffen, then Conservative Treasury Minister, gave three main reasons for the high levels of unemployment:

- A high pound (itself partly a result of the government's oil policy). A high value for the pound means that the price of British goods abroad increases and so less are sold.
- High interest rates. These push up manufacturing costs, make employers less likely to borrow to invest in new projects, and speed up bankruptcy.
- The world slump. The general depression in economic activity throughout the world means that there is less demand for our goods.

To this list should also be added the effects of the government's public spending cuts on employment in the public sector.

As more people become unemployed, they buy less goods, and as less goods are sold, even more workers become unemployed. Far from wages causing unemployment, high levels of unemployment are used as a bludgeon to hold wages down, and the demand for goods is even less. Acting alone, there is no way that individual trade unions can break this vicious circle. The only way in which unemployment can be tackled is by the labour movement taking action collectively at the political level. Yet union activities here are also a matter of controversy, and we'll look at this issue a little later.

The country needs cuts in public expenditure

'I want to say to NALGO that if they are really interested in the good of the nation and bearing in mind that, in the main, you know (and somebody has got to say this), *you represent people who produce nothing . . . ah yes, let us face the true facts*

. . . is it asking too much of you to make a little contribution to solve our nation's problems under our Labour Government.'   (Our emphasis.)

This kind of statement made by John Boyd, General Secretary of the AUEW, argues that members of NALGO, NUPE, COHSE, and indeed many white collar members of his own union, are in some way inferior to those who are directly involved in the process of producing goods. It echoes the arguments of the CBI and of many politicians who claim that hospital workers or civil servants are parasites on manufacturing industry – a luxury 'the country' cannot afford. Sometimes these arguments are taken up by public sector trade unionists themselves. 'Cut the frills, don't cut where it counts,' the COHSE journal reported, 'were amongst the slogans raised by fifty members who picketed a meeting of the Macclesfield District management team . . .' Does this mean don't cut us, cut NALGO or the CPSA?

Let's look at the issues involved and who benefits from the cuts. In some cases, high levels of public spending can help some capitalists. A large social budget means that the government may have to borrow to finance it. This may lead to higher interest rates for investors. They will get a higher return for their money from government bonds, etc., than they would if they invest elsewhere. Money follows the highest profits. Secondly, the more the government is spending, the bigger the market it creates for the products of manufacturing industry which might otherwise find problems in selling its goods.

Despite this, the CBI and both Labour and Conservative governments have insisted on the need to cut public expenditure. Their central argument has been that spending on public services diverts money that could be used to invest in productive private industry. They point out that if, for example, more building workers are employed to build hospitals, which are unproductive, i.e. unprofitable, in terms of capitalist economy, then fewer are available to build factories, which are directly productive and profitable in terms of a capitalist economy. The weakness of this argument is that this will only be the case if there is full employment, which there hasn't been in recent years.

There are two important reasons why cuts may be seen by the employers and the government as in their interest. On the one hand there is the argument – used by Denis Healey – that cuts would stop public expenditure from taking resources from industrial investment when the economy recovered and moved towards full employment. On the other, if public spending is not cut and, therefore, government borrowing *is* much greater than the money it takes in taxes, then the government may print more money. This is likely to lead to price increases as too much money chases too few goods. Then taxes will have to go up. And in this situation, workers are likely to press for higher wage increases. Employers and the last two governments wanted to avoid this. Moreover, from the employer's point of view, cuts in public expenditure increase unemployment and weaken the workers' ability to fight for higher wages and better conditions.

We have tried to simplify complicated arguments but you may still find it a bit confusing. What we are saying, in a nutshell, is that it is in the interest of private capital in general that cuts should be made, though individual employers may suffer. Cuts will make room for investment when the economy comes out of recession and also weaken the trade unions.

It is *not* a myth that the employers need cuts in public spending. It *is* a myth that such cuts are in the interest of *any* workers and that workers should support them. The Welfare State system was gained for workers and must be protected. Employers were willing to accept this in the post-war boom, and it contributed towards a healthy and educated work-force. Today, its maintenance is not in their interest. There is a clear conflict of interest here between workers and employers. It is the idea of 'the country' with a unity of interest which is a myth.

If trade unionists *do* accept that the cuts are needed, then this will cause division within the trade union movement. It will set NALGO against COHSE and the AUEW against both. In fighting against cuts we have to start from the position that workers are workers if they sell their ability to labour, whether they work at a lathe or at a drawing board, at a typewriter or in a hospital. An office worker is in no way inferior to or less important than a 'production worker'. Production would be impossible in our society without clerks, secretaries, administrators, doctors, civil servants or social workers. Any rational society would recognize that the nurse is just as socially valuable as the skilled engineer, and more essential than the shareholder or stockbroker.

Cuts in public spending mean not only the dole for those workers directly involved; less libraries, schools, social workers mean a cut in the general standard of living of all workers. In the end, they mean a weaker labour movement and they should be resisted by *all* trade unionists. The bosses may need cuts – we don't.

Unions are too involved in politics

The view is often expressed by some workers that 'politics should be kept out of trade unions'. Such a situation is impossible for several reasons.

First, if we look at the history of trade unions over the last 200 years we can see that there has been a continuous battle over the basic right of unions to exist – from the Combination Acts at the end of the eighteenth century to the Employment Act today. During this struggle, unions have fought to get governments to pass laws which permit them to organize legally. But it hasn't been easy. Parliament and the judges have often acted to restrict union organization. For most of the last century trade unions were political outlaws.

To remedy this, the TUC resolved in 1899 'to ensure that working class opinion should be represented in the House of Commons by men sympathetic with the aims and demands of the labour movement and whose candidatures are promoted by one or other of the organized movements'. Only two years later, judges ruled in the famous Taff Vale case that strike action was a civil wrong and that the union involved could be sued for damages. The Amalgamated Society of Railway Servants was forced to pay out £42,000 in

51

costs and damages. This judgement threatened the whole right to strike. It was a major influence in persuading unions to support the Labour Party when it was formed in 1906, in the hope of getting more favourable union legislation. Even today, the provisions of the Employment Act restrict several important areas of union organization. So you can see that as soon as trade unionists start discussing the rights and wrongs of the closed shop or strikes then they're talking about 'politics'. It was only through political organization that trade unions won the right to survive.

Secondly, general government policies on issues such as public spending, investment, interest rates, prices and incomes can have a direct impact on both union members' wages and employment prospects as well as on their 'social wage' – the amount of money spent on education, the health and welfare services, housing, etc., (see page 27).

Trade unions attempt to influence the policies of both Conservative and Labour governments through national discussions in forums such as the National Economic Development Council, and by campaigns on particular issues such as unemployment or the Employment Act. But the main mechanism for long term political change has been through the Labour Party.

Union involvement in the Labour Party takes place at a number of levels:

● There are regular meetings of the TUC-Labour Party Liaison Committee, consisting of representatives of the Parliamentary Labour Party, the Party's National Executive and the TUC which discuss matters of mutual interest.

● Many individual trade unions sponsor parliamentary candidates in general elections, many of whom become MPs. Such sponsorship can take a variety of forms including payment of election expenses or secretarial salaries. In the 1979 election, just under 50 per cent of the 268 Labour MPs were sponsored in this way. These included 20 sponsored by the TGWU, 16 by the NUM, 15 by the AUEW, 14 by the GMWU, 10 by the NUR, 8 by ASTMS and 7 by NUPE. While sponsored MPs are not strictly bound by the policies of their sponsoring unions, they nevertheless give these unions some parliamentary influence.

● Trade unions can exercise a more direct influence on Labour Party policy through affiliation to the party. Locally, union branches can send delegates to the management committees of constituency parties. They can only do this, however, if the union is affiliated nationally, paying a fee to the party for each union member who pays a 'political levy' in addition to their union dues. In 1977 almost six million union members were affiliated to the Labour Party in this way. However, the percentage of affiliated members varies considerably between different unions. In 1977, for example, over 95 per cent of NUM members were affiliated compared with only 37 per cent of ASTMS members. Since unions can vote at the Labour Party's annual conference on the basis of these affiliations, the casting of these union 'bloc votes' is the major factor in deciding party policy. There has been considerable controversy surrounding these 'bloc votes' since individual party members pay a much higher annual subscription than the union affiliation fee. Ways of resolving this problem are part of the current debate on Labour Party organization and democracy.

● Trade unions also have a say on the National Executive of the Labour Party which oversees the work of the party between conferences and seeks to implement conference decisions. The unions have twelve seats on the executive as of right, and also have a dominant influence, through their bloc votes, on a further six seats on the twenty-eight person executive.

So we can see that trade union influence inevitably extends beyond the workplace into society at large, in particular into the political arena via the Labour Party. Unions have had to represent the interests of their members not only as workers but also as citizens. As Bernard Dix of NUPE put it to the 1974 TUC:

'We see trade unions not simply as fruit machines in which workers put tanners to get the jackpot; we see trade unionists as agents of social change.'

For this reason, many union rule books contain broad social and economic, as well as industrial, objectives. For example, the first objective in the rules of the AUEW is: 'The control of industry in the interests of the community.' The objects of the National Union of Railwaymen include the aim: 'To work for the supersession of the capitalist system by a socialistic order of society.' While those of the TGWU encompass: 'The furtherance of political objects of any kind', as well as: 'The extension of cooperative production and distribution.' Look in your own rule book – what aims and objectives does it give for your union?

What is clear is that trade unions and politics can't be separated. Trade unionists can't behave like ostriches. Even if they try to keep away from politics, politics wont keep away from them. The only answer is to try to realize the aspirations contained in their rule books by organizing politically as well as industrially.

Chapter **Three**

Which union should you join?

If you're not in a trade union but want to join one, then choosing one can sometimes seem to be a problem. In some industries there is no choice because only one relevant union exists. But such cases are relatively rare. In most industries there are a number of unions recruiting members. Often different unions compete to recruit the same kind of worker. These are about 450 unions in this country (of which 112 are affiliated to the TUC), from the giants like the Transport and General Workers' Union (TGWU) with a membership of over two million, right down to specialized local unions such as the Teston Independent Society of Cricket Ball Makers, current membership forty-three. You will often have a choice in deciding which union to join. But obviously you can't join any union you please! Many unions limit their membership to certain categories of eligibility. For example, if you want to join the Yorkshire area of the National Union of Mineworkers you have to be employed by the Yorkshire area of the National Coal Board. If you're a cricket ball maker you will have to look elsewhere!

The aim of this chapter is to help you decide which is the most suitable union to represent you. We'll try and do the following things:

- describe the different kinds of unions;
- show which unions organize which industries;
- help you choose the relevant union if you're not already a union member.

Different kinds of unions

We briefly described the development of the trade union movement in Chapter one. But not all unions developed in the same way. The process of development, which is still going on to this day, varied greatly from industry to industry. The situation has been made more complicated by mergers and amalgamations between different kinds of unions. British unions have such a complex structure that they almost defy classification. However, it may be useful to distinguish five broad categories of union:

craft unions
vertical industrial unions
horizontal occupational unions
compact unions
general unions

What do we mean by these terms?

Craft unions

As we've seen, the earliest trade unions sprang from the trade clubs of the skilled craftsmen. These unions sought only to organize skilled workers who had served an apprenticeship. The apprenticeship system restricted entry to the trade and so limited the numbers of craftsmen in any one occupation. This scarcity of skilled labour strengthened the craft unions' bargaining position. As a result, they often exercised a high degree of control over their jobs and working conditions. These craft unions were very exclusive bodies. They made no attempt to organize the unskilled workers in their industry. Even other craftsmen were often viewed suspiciously, as potential rivals in disputes over job demarcation lines rather than as brother trade unionists. The motto of the United Society of Boilermakers summed up this highly sectional approach – 'God helps those who help themselves.' A present day example of this type of union is the Society of Lithographic Artists, Designers, Engravers and Process Workers (SLADE) which represents skilled trades in printing.

Vertical industrial unions

From the end of the nineteenth century, the job control of some craft unions was undermined by new machines which could enable semi-skilled operators to do a lot of the work formerly done by craftsmen. If this labour was unorganized and worked for low wages, it would encourage the employers to displace the craftsmen. As a result some craft unions opened their ranks to the semi-skilled and unskilled workers in their industries. They became industrial unions, seeking to organize all the workers in one industry and so strengthen their bargaining position. Such unions organize 'vertically', i.e. they seek to recruit throughout a range of occupations within one industry. Some contemporary examples are indicated in Table on page 58.

You should note that while the *aim* of these unions is to represent all grades of workers in a single industry, this is

Table 1 Examples of 'vertically' organized unions

INDUSTRIES

Coal	Steel	Railways	Post Office
underground workers	some managers	supervisors	supervisors
surface workers	clerical workers	guards	sorters
clerical workers	manual workers	porters	postmen
NUM	ISTC	NUR	UCW

UNIONS

Key: NUM – National Union of Mineworkers
ISTC – Iron and Steel Trades Confederation
NUR – National Union of Railwaymen
UCW – Union of Communications Workers (formerly Union of Post Office Workers)

only very rarely achieved in practice. On the railways, for example, many white-collar employees are members of the Transport Salaried Staff Association (TSSA) and the majority of engine drivers are in the Associated Society of Locomotive Engineers and Firemen (ASLEF).

Horizontal occupational unions

These unions organize a limited number of occupations 'horizontally', i.e. across a wide range of industries. For example, the AUEW not only recruits members in the engineering industry, but also organizes craft and maintenance workers in a variety of industries. Some examples are given in Table 2 on page 59.

Compact unions

These unions organize a limited number of occupations *within* one industry. They seek neither to organize all the workers in that industry nor to cross boundaries into other

Table 2 Examples of 'horizontally' organized unions

INDUSTRIES

		Engineering	Shipbuilding	Insurance	Furniture
U	AUEW	Fitters, drillers, millers, etc.			
N					
I	EETPU	Electricians, production workers in electrical engineering			
O					
N	APEX	Clerical workers			
S	ASTMS	Managers and technicians			

UNIONS

Key: AUEW – Amalgamated Union of Engineering Workers
EETPU – Electrical, Electronic, Telecommunications and Plumbing Union.
APEX – Association of Professional Executive Computer and Clerical Staffs.
ASTMS – Association of Supervisory Technical and Managerial Staffs.

industries. Compact unions which recruit in the industries referred to in Table 1 are as follows:

coal – National Association of Colliery Overmen, Deputies and Shotfirers (NACODS), which organize supervisory grades
steel – National Union of Blastfurnacemen
rail – TSSA and ASLEF (see page 58)
post office – Post Office Engineering Union (POEU)

General unions

For most of the nineteenth century labourers and other groups of unskilled workers were without union organization. The difficulties facing union activists were enormous – casual labour, a fluctuating labour market, a surplus of unskilled workers. But in 1889 both the dockers and gas stokers

59

set an example by forming unions. It soon became apparent that unions of unskilled workers couldn't be confined to one industry. Many gasworkers were laid off during the summer months because demand for gas was low. They got jobs in the brickmaking industry, so it was logical for the gasworkers to recruit brickworkers as well. Fear of unskilled blacklegs being employed during strikes encouraged further recruitment among other labouring groups. This prompted the dockers to attempt to enrol even farm labourers. As a result, trade unionism spread from group to group, gathering large numbers of unskilled workers from different industries into general unions.

Present day examples include the Transport and General Workers' Union and the General and Municipal Workers' Union. Because these general unions are so large and their coverage so general, some of their sections can amount to a vertical industrial union for a particular industry, e.g. the TGWU in the bus industry.

We can see that trade unions have evolved in a piecemeal sort of a way in response to changing conditions over 200 years. The result is that the structure of British trade unionism doesn't fit into a neat and tidy pattern. The main influence shaping them has not been any abstract theories but rather what was the most effective form of organization at a particular point in time. The TUC has described this situation as follows:

Just as the bargaining strength of the individual is enhanced when he combines with his fellow workers in a group at a place of employment so, on a wider plane, trade unions grew in size and extent to become whatever may be the most effective combination of workpeople to advance and protect those interests, arising from their employment, which they have in common.

Thus the structure of the trade union movement reflects whatever may at any point in time appear to be the most effective for these purposes.

Which unions organize which industries?

In this section we give information about the industries organized by some of the larger unions. It is not a comprehensive guide. For example, it ignores some large unions which are covered by a closed shop agreement throughout an entire industry, such as the National Union of Railwaymen or the National Union of Mineworkers. But it should give you a clearer picture of union coverage. (We'll discuss how you go about choosing which union to join in the next section.)

Transport and General Workers' Union The TGWU is the largest union in the country, with over two million members. It organizes in private manufacturing and service industries as well as in local authorities. It has a white-collar section. The variety of occupations among its membership is indicated by its list of National Trade Groups or Section Committees. These deal with the specific interests of the members in each group and draw up union policy on wages and conditions. They cover the following industries:

Administrative, clerical, technical and supervisory
Vehicle building and automotive
Building, construction and civil engineering
Building craft section
Chemical, rubber and oil refining
Commercial road transport
Docks, waterways, fishing etc.
Food, drink, tobacco (including agriculture and flour milling)
General workers (including textiles and man-made fibres)
Passenger services
Power and engineering
Public services and civil air transport

Amalgamated Union of Engineering Workers The AUEW is the second largest union in the country with a membership of almost one and a half million. It consists of four independent sections and we'll look at these individually.

The largest section is the *Engineering* section. It organizes among all workers in the engineering industry, men and women, unskilled, semi-skilled and skilled. It also organizes skilled maintenance workers throughout industry.

61

The *Constructional* section organizes all grades of workers in constructional engineering, i.e. construction work, bridge building etc.

The *Foundry* section is the only trade union which recruits only from foundry workers.

The *Technical, Administrative and Supervisory Section* (TASS) recruits among all staff grades in engineering and general manufacturing industry, particularly among draughtsmen but also among supervisors and foremen.

The General and Municipal Workers' Union The GMWU organizes all grades of worker throughout industry. Its membership is mainly among unskilled and semi-skilled manual workers in the following industries:

Engineering and shipbuilding
Local government and the National Health Service
Gas, electricity and water supply
Process industries such as chemicals, glass and rubber
Manufacture
Food and drink manufacture
Building material industries such as brick and cement-making
Hotel and catering

There is also a white collar section, the Managerial, Administrative, Technical and Supervisory Association (MATSA).

National Union of Public Employees NUPE organizes mainly among non-craft manual workers employed in the Health Service and by local authorities – for example, hospital porters, ambulance staff, nurses, dustbin workers, school janitors and dinner ladies.

Union of Shop, Distributive and Allied Workers USDAW is mainly a shop workers' and shop managers' union drawing much of its membership from employees of Cooperative Societies. But it has a considerable membership in industries connected with retail and wholesale shops and warehouses

– catering, laundries, hairdressing, mail order and food manufacturing.

Association of Scientific, Technical and Managerial Staffs ASTMS was formed in 1968 out of an amalgamation of two unions representing supervisory and technical staffs, mainly in the engineering industry. Since then it has been the most rapidly expanding white collar union and there have been more than thirty mergers with other unions and staff associations. It recruits non-manual staff in a very wide range of industries, including manufacturing industry, particularly engineering and chemicals, insurance and finance, electronics and data processing, medicine, including doctors, opticians, pharmacists etc. and university staff and technicians.

Electrical, Electronic, Telecommunication and Plumbing Union The EETPU covers all grades of manual workers in the industries described in its title. It has a white collar section for administrative, technical, supervisory and managerial staff in these industries.

National and Local Government Officers' Association Established in 1905, NALGO spread from local government to recruit white collar grades in the NHS, gas, electricity, water, national social services and public corporations. Affliated to the TUC in 1964 it claims to be the largest white collar union on the planet.

Union of Construction, Allied Trades and Technicians UCATT organizes mainly in the construction industry, particularly, but not only, among the more skilled workers. They also have members in shipbuilding and in maintenance departments in a wide variety of industries.

Confederation of Health Service Employees COHSE is one of the largest unions in the health service, recruiting among nurses and ancillary workers.

Association of Professional Executive Clerical and Computer Staff APEX is a white collar union recruiting supervisors, clerical and managerial staff and computer personnel in a wide variety of manufacturing industry and commerce.

National Union of Tailor and Garment Workers This is an industrial union recruiting among both manual and non-manual workers in the clothing industry and part of the textile industry.

Furniture Timber and Allied Trade Union FTAT covers all grades of manual workers in the furniture and woodworking industries.

National Union of Teachers This, the largest teachers union, organizes in schools and has always pursued equal pay given a large female membership. It also has wider educational objectives. It joined the TUC in 1970.

National Association of Schoolmasters and Union of Women Teachers Competes with NUT. Initially opposing equal pay, the NAS affiliated to the TUC in 1969 and amalgamated with UWT in 1976. Stresses qualifications and equivalent salaries.

National Union of Agricultural and Allied Workers This union not only organizes farm workers but also employees in allied trades such as chicken rearing and processing.

National Union of Hosiery and Knitwear Workers This is an industrial union for the hosiery industry. It recruits throughout Great Britain but its largest area of membership is concentrated in the Midlands.

National Union of Dyers, Bleachers and Textile Workers This union recruits throughout the textile industry. Its membership is concentrated among wool textile workers and in dyeing and finishing in Yorkshire and the North West.

Bakers, Food and Allied Workers This is an industrial union for the baking industry.

Amalgamated Textile Workers' Union This union represents workers in the spinning and weaving sections of the textile industry in Lancashire.

Civil and Public Services Association Organizes clerical secretarial and allied grades in the Civil Service, Post Office and other quasi-Civil Service departments.

Society of Civil and Public Servants Recruits executive and directing grades in the Civil Service.

Tobacco Workers' Union TWU is an industrial union for all grades of workers in the industry – manual, clerical and supervisory.

Which union do I join?

You can see from the above list that different unions organize in the same industry. You may have to make a choice, for example:
If you are a clerical worker and you work for a private company you could join either:

The Association of Professional, Executive, Clerical and Computer Staffs (APEX)

or

The Association of Scientific, Technical and Managerial Staffs (ASTMS)

or

The Administrative, Clerical, Technical and Supervisory Staffs (ACTSS a section of the Transport and General Workers Union).

or

The Managerial, Administrative, Technical and Supervisory Association (MATSA, a section of the GMWU).

If you work in a hotel you might join:

The General and Municipal Workers Union

or

The Transport and General Workers Union

If you work as an ancillary worker in a hospital you could join:

The Confederation of Health Service Employees (COHSE)

or

The National Union of Public Employees (NUPE)

Some people join NUPE because it is a large and growing union covering workers in other public services as well as the Health Service. Some people join COHSE because they believe in a union which only represents workers in the NHS. They believe that their special interests will get specific attention.

If workers decide to join a union then they have to think carefully about which is the most suitable union to represent them.

In deciding which union to join you might consider the following points:

Are other employees of your company who do similar work to you in a union? If so joining that union may give you useful support. You may work in a hotel which is part of a big chain. If workers in another part of the company are in the GMWU, you might consider joining that union. If they are in the TGWU, you may consider that union best.

If this is not so, are other kinds of workers in the company in a union? For example: if you work in an office and the shop-floor workers are in the TGWU you might feel it worthwhile to join ACTSS so you can make easier links with these workers.

Is your company non-union? If so which union recruits workers who do the same kind of work elsewhere?

Will your particular interests be looked after in a particular union? We have said that if you work in an office joining the TGWU gives you the potential support of two million workers! On the other hand some workers feel that a union organizing only office staff, like APEX, may serve their interests better.

Is the union organized in such a way as to allow ordinary members a say in union policy and the decisions which affect them?
How vigorous and effective is the union? You should not look only at what it is doing locally. Try to find out about its policies and how successful it is elsewhere.

Workers often join the first union they hear about. They then find out that this is not always the best union for them.

Perhaps the best body to contact is your local trades council. A trades council is a federation of all the unions locally, just as the Trades Union Congress (TUC) is a federation of all unions nationally. Each branch in an area sends delegates to the trades council, which usually meets monthly. It discusses and campaigns on matters of interest to local trade unionists. There are 442 trades councils in England and Wales.

You should be able to find the telephone number and address of the secretary of your trades council in the telephone book. Trades councils exist in most towns and cities. If you are in doubt about which trades council to contact, the Secretary of the Association of Trades Councils in your county will be able to advise you. If you live in Scotland and want to know which trades council covers your area, the Scottish Trades Union Congress (STUC) will be able to advise you.

Relations between unions

Because there are many trade unions in this country, they occasionally come into conflict with each other. This can take the form of demarcation disputes, about which union members should do which jobs, or jurisdictional disputes, about which unions should represent which workers. The press often exaggerate the significance of these inter-union disputes. Two points should be borne in mind.

First, although there are a very large number of unions in this country, compared with abroad, the total number of unions is declining as a result of mergers. It was 1323 in 1900, now it's about 460. More important, almost 80 per cent of union membership is contained in the fourteen largest unions.

Second, on average, *less than 5 per cent* of strikes are inter-union disputes.

It is in the general interests of the trade union movement for there to be harmonious and stable relationships between unions. Inter-union squabbles can play into the hands of hostile employers. The employers can play off two unions against each other and follow a 'divide and conquer' policy. This is often especially true when unions are organizing in a new workplace and haven't yet won recognition from the employer. Competition between two unions can sometimes result in neither organizing successfully.

Over the years, unions, through the TUC, have sought to avoid such situations. A TUC booklet 'TUC Disputes: Principles and Procedures' describes the steps which have been taken.

In 1939 the Bridlington Congress adopted a series of recommendations designed to minimize disputes between unions over membership questions. They laid down the procedures by which the TUC dealt with complaints by one organization against another and considered disputes between unions. They were drawn up because trade unionists recognized that, in situations where more than one union was capable of representing a particular grade of worker, it was necessary to prevent the indiscriminate proliferation of unions if stable and rational trade union structures and collective bargaining machinery were to be developed. Their existence has also prevented the instability that would occur if breakaway unions were formed, or if groups of workers were able to move on a whim from one union to another.

These procedures, which had come to be known as the Bridlington Principles and which were set out in the booklet 'Relations between Unions', were supplemented in 1969 by further recommendations adopted by the Special Congress held at Croydon.

The Bridlington Principles put some limits on workers' freedom of choice as to which union they may join. For example, Principle 5 states:

No union shall commence organizing activities at any establishment or undertaking in respect of any grade or grades of workers in which another union has the majority of workers employed and negotiates wages and conditions, unless by arrangement with that union.

This limits *where* a union can organize. There are also limits on *who* unions can admit to membership under Principle 2:

Principle 2

No one who is or has recently been a member of any affiliated union should be accepted into membership in another without enquiry of his present or former union. The present or former union shall be under an obligation to reply within 21 days of the enquiry, stating:

(a) Whether the applicant has tendered his resignation;
(b) Whether he is clear on the books;
(c) Whether he is under discipline or penalty;
(d) Whether there are any other reasons why the applicant should not be accepted.

If the present or former union objects to the transfer, and the enquiring union considers the objection to be unreasonable, the enquiring union shall not accept the applicant into membership but shall maintain the status quo with regard to membership. If the problem cannot be mutually resolved it should be referred to the TUC for adjudication.

A union should not accept an applicant into membership if no reply has been received 21 days after the enquiry, but in such circumstances a union may write again to the present or former union, sending a copy of the letter to the head office of the union if the correspondence is with a branch, stating that if no reply is received within a further 14 days they intend to accept the applicant into membership. Where the union to which application is being made is dealing directly with the head office of the present or former union, a copy of this communication may be sent to the TUC.

This means that branch secretaries have to check on new applicants to their union if they have recently been in another union. People can't switch unions willy-nilly.

You will have to bear these points in mind when choosing which union to join and when trying to recruit fellow workers into it. There may be unions already in existence at your workplace but you are not yet a member of any of them. You should find out if any agreement exists between them as to which one is the relevant one for you.

Further reading

If you want to read more on union structure then dip into the relevant chapters in the books by Clegg, Hyman, Coates and Topham in the reading list at the end of this book. In A. Marsh, *Trade Union Handbook* (Gower Press, 1980) you will find a comprehensive list of the basic details and addresses of trade unions in Britain. This is very expensive but you should find it in a reference library.

Chapter **Four**

How trade unions work

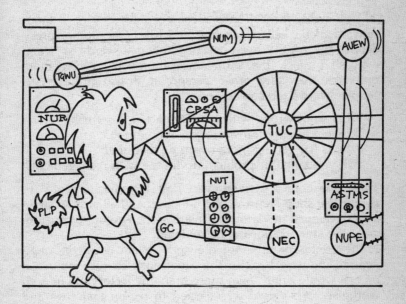

So far we've looked at the reasons why we have trade unions, the arguments for joining one (we hope we've convinced you!) and which types of unions organize which industries. But if you're new to trade unionism, it's important that you understand exactly how unions operate. In this chapter, we'll look at the 'nuts and bolts' of trade unions and how they fit together. We'll examine:

- shop-stewards and what they do;
- the union branch and what it's for;
- union constitutions and how policies are made;
- relations between members and union officials;
- the role of the TUC in the trade union movement.

The shop-steward

'I'm all right, Jack!' That's most people's idea of a shop-steward. Peter Sellers playing Fred Kite. One former president of the AUEW even described shop-stewards as 'werewolves'! In fact, the shop-steward probably solves more problems than any other person in British industry. A shop-steward's job consists of:

'What went wrong with my pay packet this week?'
'Why am I being transferred to another job?'
'Why is Joe getting more overtime than me?'
'Will you take this problem up for me with management?'

These questions are asked every day. Who has to deal with them? The shop-steward. We'll look first of all at how stewards developed in various industries, then go on to consider what the steward does in more detail.

The origins of the shop-steward system lie in the engineering industry back in the nineteenth century. A union branch would often cover more than one factory. So in each workplace, a steward was elected to recruit members and collect the members' dues. It was during the First World War that shop-stewards came into the forefront of industrial relations. The government's war effort demanded that unions abandon their traditional working practices and apprenticeship regulations. In support of the government, the union leaders accepted these proposals. But this created lots of problems in the factories. The changes brought about by wartime production required lots of day to day negotiation. The shop-stewards became the natural leaders in these workshop negotiations. The stewards from each factory linked up into committees in some of the large towns, such as Glasgow and Sheffield, to coordinate their activity. The importance of the munitions industry gave the shop-stewards considerable bargaining power. The case of Leonard Hargreaves, a skilled fitter who was called up to fight in the trenches, is a good example. There was an agreement that skilled men would not be called up before the unskilled 'dilutees'.

'The Shop-Stewards' Committee of Sheffield demanded that he be released in line with government assurances and a mass meeting held under its auspices on 13 November (1916) threatened to strike unless its demands were complied with. On the 15th, Hargreaves was released from the army.'
   J. B. Jefferys *The Story of the Engineers: 1800–1945* (AEU, 1945)

In the depression years between the wars, mass unemployment reduced the bargaining power of trade unionists in the workshops. The shop-steward was often the first to be sacked. It was an irony of history that some of the leaders of the shop-stewards' movement during the First World War were to become the leaders of the unemployed workers' movement of the 1920s and '30s. However, during the last war and the period of full employment in the post war years, shop-stewards' organization once more revived. For example, between 1947 and 1955, the number of AEU (forerunner of the AUEW) shop-stewards in companies belonging to the Engineering Employers' Federation increased by 24 per cent; between 1955 and 1961 by 39 per cent.

Shop-stewards throughout manufacturing industry negotiated about payment systems, as well as a wide range of other issues. They were often able to extend their workshop control by establishing informal 'custom and practice' arrangements and to defend this control when necessary by short unofficial strikes. In the 1960s, managements attempted to regain some of this control by 'buying out' custom and practice and establishing formal procedures through productivity deals. But the local negotiations which these deals involved also stimulated the growth of shop-steward organization.

By the 1970s, stewards were developing outside the manufacturing sector. The introduction of local incentive schemes

73

in local government and the health service also demanded detailed negotiations in the workplace. This led to the recognition of shop-stewards in hospitals and local authority employment. The dramatic expansion of union membership among white collar workers was also accompanied by the development of 'staff representatives' or office shop-stewards. In 1960, it had been estimated that the number of stewards in British industry was between 100,000 and 200,000. By 1975, the TUC estimated the figure was about 300,000.

In some cases, trade unions took an active part in encouraging the development of shop-stewards and integrating them into the union structure. NUPE, with many members in the Health Service and local government, authorized the election of shop-stewards for the first time in 1970. When the union's constitution was revised in the mid-70s, stewards automatically became members of branch committees. NALGO, representing many grades of local government white collar workers, also only developed a shop-steward system in the mid-70s. A survey of members in one large branch in Sheffield showed a majority felt they were better informed and the union more effective as a result. (The development of shop-stewards is dealt with further in a companion volume in this series, *Unions and change since 1945* by C. Baker and P. Caldwell.)

Shop-steward is the term most commonly used for workplace representatives but in some industries other terms are used. In some white collar unions it's 'office rep.'; in the draughtsman's union it's 'corresponding member'; in the railways, 'local departmental committee (LDC) rep.'; in the printing industry it's 'father of the chapel'. However, the essential features of the job are the same.

Shop-stewards are not full-time paid officials of the union. They do the job voluntarily and are usually elected by the group of people they represent in the workplace or at the union branch meeting. For example, look at Rule 41 of the General and Municipal Workers' Union in this extract:

Rule 41 – Shop-Stewards

1. Shop-Stewards shall be appointed, or elected, by the members employed where it is deemed necessary, and subject to approval by the Branch Committee, or the Regional Secretary if more than one Branch is involved.

2. Appointments shall be by any of the following methods, whichever is the most suitable in the particular case:

  (a) by a majority vote on a show of hands, or by ballot, of the members concerned at the place of employment;

  (b) by a majority vote on a show of hands at a Branch meeting;

  (c) by common consent among the members concerned that the office shall be filled by a member appointed by the Regional Secretary.

  (d) Shop-Stewards may elect one of their number at the place of employment, as Convenor.

Because the shop-steward is an ordinary worker, he is in daily contact with the members he represents. He is meant to act as their spokesman and look after their interests. If his members feel he isn't doing this properly they can elect a new steward at election time. In many workplaces, stewards come up for election each year. For example, Rule 22 of the National Union of Public Employees states:

Stewards shall hold office for one year and shall be eligible for re-election. Annual elections of stewards shall coincide with the annual meeting of the Branch and stewards shall hold office for the same period as Branch Officers as set out in Union Rules.

The size of the shop-steward's 'constituency' – that is, the members he represents, can vary enormously. It may be less than ten, it may be several hundred. The number of shop-stewards in a particular workplace will depend on:

- the number of union members;
- the variety of occupations;
- where the members work and the layout of the workplace;
- how the shift system operates.

For example, if there are five members in the packing department and six members in the dispatch department next door, one steward may represent both groups of workers. If there are ninety members in the assembly shop, there may be two or three stewards in this one department. Normally, a shop-steward represents members of his own union. If there are members of another union in the same workplace, they will usually have their own steward to represent them.

If there are several shop-stewards in a workplace, they will often form a committee and elect a convenor. He will be responsible for calling meetings and acting as the leader of the stewards in negotiations with management. Where there are stewards from more than one union, they will often form a joint shop-stewards' committee with its own convenor. Such a committee is an important way of coordinating the work of the different unions in a workplace. The structure of the steward's organization in a large factory is outlined in Figure 4. For the same reasons, shop-stewards from different workplaces owned by the same employer often organize a combine committee to link up the various joint shop-stewards' committees.

The job of the shop-steward is a varied and often difficult one. In fact, its about ten jobs rolled into one! These will vary between unions and in different workplaces, but a shop-steward's main functions are:

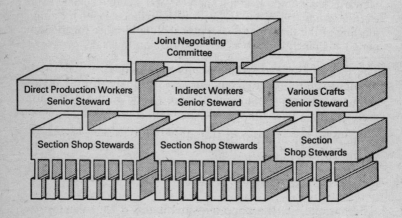

Figure 4. Typical shop steward's organization in a large factory

● To recruit members into the union, especially new starters at the workplace.

● To collect members' union dues. If these are deducted from wages automatically by the employer and paid directly to the union – the 'check-off' system – he should ensure that it operates efficiently.

● To take up members' grievances with management. For example, if a member feels that he's always getting the worst jobs, then the steward will look into the case and take it up if it is justified. However, not all members' complaints will be genuine grievances against the employer. Each case needs to be investigated.

● To defend members if management are attempting to discipline them. For example, if a union member is being warned about bad timekeeping because his wife's ill, the steward will look into the full facts of the case and argue them before management.

● To negotiate on wages and conditions. The steward may do this along with his fellow stewards or with the union full-time official. You should note that not all workplaces have local negotiations about wages.

● To represent his members if they are exposed to health and safety hazards. In some workplaces there will be a separate trade union health and safety representative elected by the members, but he will need to work closely with the shop-steward.

To carry out all these tasks effectively requires a lot of time. If the steward's trade union is *recognized* by management for representation and negotiating purposes, then the shop-steward is legally entitled to time off the job with pay to do these things. The details of how this operates are described in the later chapter on 'Building your organization'. Every steward should make sure that he always has handy copies of all relevant agreements, a shop-stewards' handbook and the union rules.

The basic job of the shop-steward is to act as the spokesman for the members and to represent their interests. This isn't always easy. The members may be divided amongst themselves. For example, some may want to resist management proposals for reducing the workforce. Others may be in favour of accepting them because they want to collect redundancy pay. The shop-steward has to act as a leader and give guidance on such issues.

Sometimes the steward's job is made more complicated by the fact that he's not *only* a spokesman for his members. He's also an official of his union and responsible to it. For example, you'll notice that in the rule of the General and Municipal Workers' Union quoted earlier, the shop-steward acts under the jurisdiction of his branch. In the Engineering section of the AUEW, the shop-steward is responsible to the district committee. Most unions have similar rules. Problems can sometimes arise for the steward if there is a conflict between his members and the union. Say the union bans overtime working to create the need for more jobs. Some members may want to continue working overtime to maintain their earnings. There's no easy answer to this. The steward should try to persuade his members to follow union policy. If the members don't agree with the policy, they can go to their branch meeting and try and get it changed.

The union branch

The branch is the basic unit of union organization. Every union member belongs to a branch. If a new branch is being formed, union rule books often specify that there must be a minimum number of members to justify setting one up. For example, in the GMWU and the NUR there has to be twenty members, in the Transport and General Workers it's fifty.

In some situations, the branch is a grouping of workers who live in the same area. They may work at a variety of different workplaces and even in different industries, depending on the coverage of the union concerned. This is known as a geographical branch. In other cases, the branch will cover all the union members in one workplace – a workplace branch. If you join a union which is not recognized at your workplace, it is probable that you will join the first kind of branch.

Branches usually have standing orders – rules under which the business of the branch is conducted. Branches are administered by the branch committee. This will include:

- a chairman, who is responsible for conducting the branch meetings according to the standing orders;
- a secretary, who writes and receives letters on behalf of the branch, records branch decisions in the minutes and deals with membership applications;
- a treasurer, who is responsible for making sure the members dues are collected and paid into the union's bank account.

The branch is the forum where members can discuss the problems of their workplace, the running of the union and also broader political and social issues of interest to trade unionists generally. Branches will often send delegates to other bodies in the union – these are discussed a little later in the chapter. Branches can also affiliate and send delegates to other bodies such as trades councils and the local branch of the Labour Party. These delegates will report on what has gone on at these bodies to the branch meeting.

We'll look in more detail at the mechanics of *how* branch meetings are conducted in a later chapter. The main point to note here is that the branch is the starting point from which members participate in the democratic running of their union. If branches are poorly attended and become unrepresentative, this poses a problem for union democracy. Unfortunately, low attendance at branch meetings is common throughout the trade union movement. Sometimes only a dozen or so members out of several hundred will bother to turn up. Why are branch meetings badly attended? What can be done about it?

Some branches have *boring* meetings, carrying out the same routine business month after month, in cold rooms sitting on hard chairs, displaying a general air of unfriendliness to any new members. This is fatal. So, make the meetings interesting and lively. Invite visiting speakers such as the full-time official to address the branch on current union issues such as the annual wage claim. Elect a branch education officer to organize short talks on topical items, such as the probable impact of the microchip on your industry. Bodies such as the Workers' Educational Association, to which union branches can affiliate, will prove helpful here. A comfortable setting such as a social or Labour club will often help to encourage a sociable atmosphere at branch meetings. Some branches even provide a pint of free beer to encourage members to attend! Branch committee members should make a point of welcoming and introducing new members to the meeting.

The content of branch meetings may seem *irrelevant* to some members. This problem often occurs in geographical branches with members in a large number of workplaces. Most of their problems are dealt with by the shop-steward organization at their own workplace. For this reason, its important that shop-stewards are involved in branch activities. Otherwise, there's a danger of a split between the union inside and outside the workplace. For example, NUPE's Rule 18 states that all shop-stewards in a branch shall be members of the branch committee. Moreover:

'The Branch Committee shall:
   (a) coordinate local negotiations conducted by union stewards in the Branch;
   (b) establish and maintain adequate representation of members' interests by Union Stewards in the sections and workplaces covered by the Branch;
   (c) report to Union Stewards in the Branch any matters concerning the members they represent;'

There is much less likelihood of a separation between stewards and the branch in workplace branches. On the other hand it can be argued that geographical branches encourage the interaction of members from different workplaces who can learn a great deal from each other. There is less of a danger of only concentrating on workplace issues and ignoring the wider problems which working people face.

Some branch meetings are held at awkward times. It's often difficult for shift workers or women with heavy family

How to kill your Branch
in eleven easy stages

1 Don't go to the meetings.

2 If you go, arrive late.

3 If the weather is good say 'It's too fine an evening to be sitting cooped up inside,' then watch television.

4 If the weather is bad say 'I can't go out on a night like this,' then watch television.

5 If you do attend a meeting, find fault with the work of the officials and others.

6 Never accept an office, as it is easier to criticize than to act.

7 Complain loudly if you are not appointed on a committee; but if you are, do not attend committee meetings.

8 If asked by the chairman to give your opinion regarding some important matter, tell him you have nothing to say. Bore the backside off everyone later on in the bar by telling them exactly what should have been done.

9 Do nothing more than is absolutely necessary. When other members roll up their sleeves and willingly use their ability to help matters along, howl that the branch is run by a clique.

10 Having elected your chairman and secretary, begin to tell everybody they are a couple of power-mad careerists.

11 When asked to argue for some difficult action, refuse to do so on the grounds that the members are too apathetic.

commitments to attend. The branch should consider when the most convenient time is, taking the needs of *all* the members into account. Some workplace branches have better attendances because the meetings are held at the end of a shift or between shifts. If there are women members in the branch the branch committee should arrange a crèche, say, on a Saturday morning, so that they can bring the kids.

Social activities such as outings and dances can help to generate interest in the branch, not just among members but also their families.

Union activists need to continually educate the members on their role in the union. If they don't show up at the branch, they deprive themselves of any say in union affairs.

Union constitutions and union policy

In this section, we'll consider two main questions:

How are unions governed?
How are union policies made?

In the simplest situation, union members in their branches elect a national executive to run the union and implement policy. The policies of the union will be decided by the annual conference consisting of delegates elected from the branches. In practice, and particularly in larger unions, there are variations in this basic framework. The exact structures will vary from union to union, but generally there are several levels of policy- and decision-making between the rank and file branch members and the union leadership. These consist of delegated committees based on either geographical or industrial divisions. Here are three examples.

In the *Engineering section* of the *Amalgamated Union of Engineering Workers*, district committees are elected from the members in the branches and from the district's shop-stewards. This committee oversees negotiations on wages and conditions and provides a forum in which its members, many of them senior stewards, can coordinate action in the locality. The districts are grouped into twenty-six organizing divisions and districts send delegates to divisional committees. Each divisional committee elects two delegates to the National Committee. This is the highest policy-making body in the union. It meets annually and corresponds to the 'conference' in most other unions. The implementation of the decisions made by the National Committee is the responsibility of the Executive Council. This body consists of the union's President and seven full-time executive members who are elected from seven national executive divisions. The main links between the executive and the branches are the district committees. With the executive's approval, these committees can initiate strike action and impose district levies to support local disputes.

The *Transport and General Workers' Union* has developed a combination of geographical and sectional representation, since it covers members in a wide variety of industries. The work of the union's branches is coordinated administratively through district committees or industrially through regional trade group committees. In either case, the committee members are elected from the branches. The work of these committees is overseen by eleven regional committees whose members are normally elected from the district and trade group committees. The particular industrial interests of the various sections of the members are looked after by national trade group committees. The governing body of the union is the General Executive Council. This consists of twenty-six members elected from the regions and one representative from each national trade group – a total of thirty-nine, all of whom are lay members, not full-time officials. The highest policy making body is the Biennial Delegate Conference. Its 1100 or so delegates are nominated from branches and elected by ballot of the regional trade groups.

In the *National Union of Public Employees*, the structure is more complicated. If all the members in a branch are employed by a single local authority or NHS district authority, then the branch is known as a district branch; other branches are called non-district branches. The branches coordinate local negotiations carried on by their shop-stewards. In each local authority or health service district, there is a NUPE branch district committee consisting of the secretaries, chairmen and shop-stewards in either local government or the NHS of all the non-district branches in the district. In the case of district branches, the branch committee is also the branch district committee. The country is divided into ten divisions which are further subdivided into areas. In each area there are area committees covering local government, the NHS, water services, and universities. They are made up of delegates from each branch district committee covering the relevant service within the area. Within each division there is an annual divisional conference made up of delegates from the branch district committees. Between these conferences, union policy in the division is administered by the divisional council which is made up of representatives from the area committees. National committees, elected from either the areas or divisions, exist for the four main areas of membership – local government, NHS, the water service and universities. National policy for all sections of the union is made by the national conference which is held every two years. The general management of the union is carried out by the executive council whose twenty-six members are elected by branch ballot.

These examples of three unions, each of which has evolved under historical and industrial circumstances, give some idea of the variety of union constitutions. There are no easy or simple answers about which kind of union structure is best. At the TGWU Biennial Conference there are over a thousand delegates. At the AUEW (Engineering Section) National Committee there are fifty-two. The TGWU member may say: 'Our conference is more representative because it's bigger.' The AUEW member might reply: 'Our national committee meets more frequently and is smaller, so there can be much fuller discussion.' Who's right? In short, both are. No particular union structure has a monopoly on democracy. The important thing is the general principle of allowing the members to be actively involved.

Do you know how your own union operates? From the rule book or other union literature you should be able to find out the following points:

- how your national executive is elected;
- how the delegates to conference are chosen;
- if there are district or regional committees;
- how your general secretary is chosen.

You will also need to know the mechanics of how policies are actually made within this constitutional framework. For example, how are motions discussed at annual conference? There will probably be a timetable laid down for this each year. In ASTMS, for example, the procedure for organizing the Annual Delegate Conference in May begins in the previous September when the union's head office circulates the timetable for conference preparations to the branches. This typically proceeds as follows:

- motions are invited on 23 October, each branch and divisional council can submit up to two motions;
- the closing date for these motions is 4 December;
- nominations for conference delegates are invited on 18 December;
- the preliminary agenda (i.e. the list of motions submitted) is issued by 13 January, along with invitations for amendments to the motions and for divisional councils to submit their priorities for discussion;
- the closing date for the submission of each branch's December financial return on membership, on which the size of the branch's conference delegation is based, is 21 January;
- the closing date for the nomination of delegates is 12 February;
- amendments to motions have to be submitted by 19 February;
- the final agenda, the national executive committee's annual report, and the list of priority subjects is circulated on 26 March;
- the programme of business and the first report of the Standing Orders Committee are issued by 16 April;
- conference materials are issued to delegates and visitors from 30 April;
- the actual conference itself takes place on 16–18 May,

when the report, the motions and amendments are discussed and debated.

This may seem very technical and bureaucratic. The procedure will vary from union to union. But making sure that issues are fairly discussed and decided upon in a large, democratic organization is never easy. Within this framework, the individual union member in his branch can put forward a conference motion. If the branch votes to support it, it goes forward for further discussion. Other members in their branches can propose amendments. For example, look at the following extract from the 1980 ASTMS conference agenda on the controversial issue of Labour Party constitutional change:

Political Activity

72. Manchester South 127

This Annual Conference instructs the NEC that to further the decisions of the 1979 Labour Party Conference taken in Brighton, the Parliamentary Committee of ASTMS members support the following:
- (A) The decision of the inquiry into the set up of the Labour Party organization and finance.
- (B) That the Prime Minister be elected by an electorial college.
- (C) Mandatory re-selection of MPs.
- (D) The NEC of the Labour Party issue of the manifesto of socialist strategy for long term realization objectives.
- (E) Also, ASTMS financial supported MPs should be full time members of the House of Commons and not engaged on other projects financial or industrial outside Parliament.
- (F) And when 65 years of age, retire at the end of the sitting Parliament, join the ranks of the OAPs in order to sustain pressure on the Government to realize that pensions should allow people to live above the line of poverty, not on it.

Amendment: MERSEYSIDE HEALTH SERVICE 159
After 'members' (Lines 3 and 4) insert 'be encouraged to'.
In (A) delete 'The decision' and substitute 'a debate within ASTMS on the decisions'.
In (B) delete 'Prime Minister' and substitute 'leader of the Labour Party'.

Delete 'Electorial' and substitute 'electoral'. Delete paragraphs (D) (E) and (F).

Amendment: SHEFFIELD CENTRAL 597
Delete A.
Substitute 'workplace Labour Party Branches should be introduced'.
Delete B.
Substitute 'election of leader by Labour Party Conference'.
In F delete all after 'Parliament' in line two.

Amendment: AVON 461
Line 9 after '(C) Mandatory re-selection of MPs' add 'by the general management committees of the Constituency Labour Parties concerned'.

Amendment: BRADFORD 199
In (C), line 9 after MPs add: 'selection or re-selection of MPs to be carried out by management of Constituency Labour Parties.'

Amendment: LEEDS 507
Line 9, add 'By General Management Committees of Constituency Labour Parties.'

Amendment: EXECUTIVE STAFFS BRANCH 623
Sub-Clause B: delete 'Prime Minister' in line one, replace with 'Leader of the Parliamentary Labour Party'. Add at end of clause 'as put to 1979 Labour Party Conference in Composite Resolution 18'.

Amendment: N. LONDON MEDICAL 42
Delete clauses (E) and (F).

Amendment: AVON 461
Line 15, after 'Parliament' add 'with their voting record on major pieces of legislation recorded in the ASTMS Journal'.

To ensure that conference does not endlessly debate broadly similar motions the standing orders committee which is responsible for the conference organization will discuss ways of merging or 'compositing' them with the various movers. Once the conference delegates have voted in favour of a motion, then it becomes the policy of the union.

In theory at least, the principles of delegated committees and democratic policy-making are common to all unions. In practice, the situation is not always so clearly defined. Union leaders and executives often exert a very considerable influence over lay conferences by virtue of their prestige, power and expertise. For example, the platform of the TGWU's Biennial Delegate Conference was only defeated twice, on fairly minor issues, between 1945 and 1977. The BDC of 1977 was exceptional in that the conference voted in favour of a return to free collective bargaining against the advice of the then General Secretary, Jack Jones. Previously, successive general secretaries had carried the conferences with them. But such dramatic reverses are relatively rare at union conferences. More commonly, conference arrangements committees will seek to restrict the time available to motions disapproved of by union executives, or else dilute them by compositing them with other motions.

Moreover, once policies have been made by conference, they still have to implemented by the executive and full-time officials. We'll now look at what control the membership exercises over this process.

Members and officials

At the end of the nineteenth century, two famous historians of the trade union movement pointed to the pressures on full-time officials:

Whilst the points at issue no longer affect his own earnings or conditions of employment, any disputes between his members and their employers increase his work and add to his worry . . . His manner to his members . . . undergoes a change . . . Unconsciously biased by distaste for the hard and unthankful work which a strike entails, he finds himself in small sympathy with the men's demands and eventually arranges a compromise on terms distasteful to a large section of his members.
Sidney and Beatrice Webb *History of Trade Unionism*

The nature of the full-time official's job also tends to make his ideas more conservative. He may not wish to risk a sectional strike or a strike over what he sees as a small issue because of the impact on union funds or the impact on employment elsewhere in a company or industry. The members may feel differently. The full-time official as a professional negotiator is predisposed to become attuned to the logic of collective bargaining. He may become used to 'trading off' issues with his fellow professionals on the other side of the bargaining table. As the official moves up the union ladder, pressures to accept arguments about the 'national interest' may become more appealing. Moss Evans is in a different position from the TGWU assembly-line worker. He may therefore act differently.

This does not mean that all officials are 'sell-outs'. What we are talking about are *pressures*. The other main pressure on the official comes from the members. In the end, if they do not accept his policies he will have to come into line, although this may be in the long term rather than the short term. Similarly, left-wing officials can be limited in what they want to achieve by more conservative members. You can't blame union defeats simply on the officials or on a lack of leadership. You need to look at the members, and how willing they are to support or pressurize their officials, first.

This is not to suggest that union officials do not work hard. Indeed part of the problem is that they have a variety of jobs to do. First, they are *organizers*. They have to recruit members to the union and service those who are already members. They do this by assisting with guidance and information on a union policy, by attending branch meetings, by helping to run strikes, by organizing educational meetings. They are also *negotiators*, who either assist shop-stewards in bargaining with their employer or who conduct negotiations on the members' behalf. Such negotiations may range from drawing up and bargaining about the pay claim affecting thousands of members to defending an individual member threatened with dismissal. And if the member is sacked, then the official may have to present the case before an industrial tribunal. Finally, the official is also an *administrator*, reporting to the union's head office, liaising with other unions or the regional TUC and generally overseeing the work of the union in the district.

The number of members an official has to cover may vary greatly from union to union. In 1966, for example, an official of USDAW, the shop workers' union was responsible for less than 2000 members on average; in the TGWU it was just less than 4000 while in the AEU it was 6800. Unions with a long tradition of shop-steward organization and a high level of membership activity may need less assistance from full-time officers than others. There is no simple answer as to when members should call in their official. Active trade unionists should try to handle their workplace problems without always phoning the full-time official first; but when you think you need the official's help call him or her in. You'll find this happens far more often when you're getting organized than when you've built up a well-established union organization in your workplace.

So you can see that union officials are not only busy people, they are inevitably subject to a variety of sometimes conflicting pressures: from different sections of their membership; from their senior officials and executive committees; from the burden of administrative duties, and so on. To ensure that the interests of their members and the carrying out of union policy remain of paramount importance, unions have evolved a number of controls.

Elections

The most effective control is for officials to be subject to regular re-election. In some unions, local full-time officers are elected by the members. In the AUEW, all full-time officials must also come up for re-election. This makes them, like the shop-steward, accountable to the members they represent. However, the trend in many unions, particularly white collar ones, is for officials to be appointed to their jobs by the union executive. Since they don't come up for election or re-election the members can't have any *direct* influence on their actions.

This problem is equally relevant to union general secretaries. Of those who are elected, most are elected until they retire. Of the major unions, only the AUEW and the EETPU demand periodic re-election. There is usually provision in the rules for them to be sacked if they do something really outrageous, but in practice this very rarely happens. Some people argue that if they're in the job for life, union leaders can get out of touch with their rank and file members. One way round this would be for the general secretary to stand for regular re-election on his record of leadership.

The basis of union elections is also a controversial subject. In some unions they are conducted in the branches. One objection to this is that if branches are badly attended, there will be a low return. Until 1972, the AUEW conducted their elections this way and there was an average voting turnout of less than 10 per cent. Sometimes low turnouts are concealed by the votes of all branch members being cast in a block, whether they're actually at the meeting or not. But this can hardly be called very democratic. In other unions, postal ballots are held. In some cases this leads to an increase in voting, but not by a dramatic amount. There is usually about a 20 per cent response rate in the EETPU and around 30 per cent in the Engineering section of the AUEW postal ballots. Objections to this method are based on the fact that the member votes as an isolated individual who may have been the target of concerted media campaigns rather than as an informed member participating in a collective group; on the high costs involved; and because of the difficulties in compiling accurate and up to date electoral registers. The problems connected with both branch and postal ballots are avoided to a considerable extent by workplace ballots. In the National Union of Mineworkers, for example, turn-outs of between 70–80 per cent are achieved in pithead ballots.

Supervision of officials by elected executives

An important democratic control in many unions is for an elected national executive to oversee the work of the national officials. In some unions, such as the AUEW and the EETPU, the members of this elected committee themselves become full-time officials. In others, such as the TGWU and NUPE, the executive is made up of lay members. Neither method is perfect. A small full-time executive may become out of touch with the members and identify with the union's other full-time officials. A lay executive will have less experience and meet less frequently. This may prevent it being an effective check on full-time officers.

Consulting the members

One way for union officials to ensure that they are carrying out the wishes of their members is to consult them. It is now normal practice for TGWU negotiators to refer back new agreements to the members involved for ratification. In some union rulebooks, ballots of the members will be held before the executive can call a strike or to agree to national wage negotiations.

In recent years, there has been a general push for greater lay involvement in running union affairs. This is surely a healthy sign. It is in part a result of the growth in day to day contact of shop-stewards with their members. This pressure has been reflected in unions such as the TGWU, the GMWU and NUPE adapting their constitutions to allow greater participation by lay members. Others have been slow or resistant to change. Rules revision conferences are held at fairly infrequent intervals. In the TGWU it's normally only every six years, in the AUEW every five years. It's important that you find out from your rule book how your own rules are revised. Because if you're dissatisfied with any of the workings of your own union, it's through rules revision conferences that you can change things.

The TUC

If you're a union member, your union will very likely be affiliated to the TUC. Hardly a week goes by without the TUC General Secretary or a member of the General Council appearing on the television or the radio. We've already noted the importance of the TUC in influencing government policies. But the popular image of all-powerful TUC leaders is far from accurate. It's important that you know just how the TUC works and what its powers are, because it represents the collective voice of the trade union movement in this country.

There are 112 unions, including all the major ones, which affiliate to the TUC by paying a fee for each member per year. (In 1978, this annual fee was twenty pence per member.) These affiliated unions represent more than 50 per cent of the working population and over 90 per cent of all trade union members.

The TUC's main policy-making body is the annual Congress, to which each affiliated union sends delegates on the basis of one for every 5000 members. Each union can send in up to two motions and the TUC's General Council (see below) can submit three. Motions and amendments are either decided on by a show of hands, or more formally by a 'card vote'. This means the union delegations vote on the basis of one vote for every thousand affiliated members that they represent.

In addition to voting on policy resolutions, Congress also discusses the annual report of the General Council, a lengthy document of several hundred pages describing the work of the Council and its committees over the previous year. If the congress delegates are dissatisfied with any actions of the council, they can censure it by 'referring back' that section of the report. On occasions, Congress has overturned General Council decisions. For example, in 1971, the General Council's 'recommendation' to unions not to register under the Conservative Government's Industrial Relations Act was changed to an 'instruction' by Congress. Such instances are fairly rare, however, perhaps because union delegations tend to be dominated by full-time officials. Sometimes union leaders have cast their union's card vote against the advice of their union delegations. Such problems can't be resolved by the TUC. They can only be dealt with by campaigning for greater democratic accountability within individual unions.

Congress also elects the forty-one members of the General Council which is the TUC's governing body between annual congresses. General Council members are nominated from nineteen groups, eighteen industrial and one women's, but are elected by all congress delegates. This means that the larger unions can effectively determine the composition of Council. One criticism of the make up of the General Council is that some industries are disproportionately represented. For example, the mining and railway groups, with a membership of less than 300,000 members each, both have two seats, while the Civil Service and Post Office group, with almost 950,000 members, has only three seats. The distribution of seats is reallocated from time to time; prior to 1977 for example, the Civil Service group had only two seats. Suggestions that a seat on the General Council should automatically be given to unions over a certain size, with a proportional increase in the number of seats according to membership, have been rejected on the grounds that this would enlarge the Council to an unwieldy extent. Against this, some smaller unions claim that the make up of the Council is unrepresentative at present.

The General Council meets monthly and oversees the work of its standing committees, which include the finance and general purposes, international, education, social insurance and industrial welfare, employment policy and organization, economics, and equal rights. These are backed up by the TUC's 120 or so full-time specialist staff. Congress resolutions are referred to these committees for detailed examination, and recommendations for action are then made to the General Council. The action which the Council then takes is reported on for approval to the next Congress.

Although the TUC provides a forum for unions to develop common policies, neither Congress nor the Council can directly override the independence of the constituent unions. Implementing policy largely depends on reaching agreement among the members of the General Council, who in the main are union general secretaries. Note that the General Council cannot instruct a union to call its members out on strike. The Council's duties and powers are laid out in the TUC's Rules and Standing Orders. Rule 8 states that the Council should 'where possible coordinate industrial action'. Rule 11 demands that unions keep the Council informed of major disputes, but unless requested, the Council won't intervene if there is a prospect of a negotiated settlement. Should negotiations break down, the Council is empowered to offer advice and assistance, and, if this advice is accepted by the union, organize 'all moral and material support as the circumstances of the dispute may appear to justify'. Should the union refuse the General Council's advice, this would be reported to the next Congress to decide on any disciplinary action.

The TUC's relationship to individual unions in industrial disputes is therefore primarily to advise and coordinate. No central strike fund exists and policies cannot be directly imposed. If the circumstances are sufficiently serious, the General Council can convene a national conference of union executives with powers to decide action on a particular issue. This was the procedure used to call the General Strike in 1926. Special Congresses have also been called in recent years. For example, in March 1971, a special meeting of Congress agreed on a plan of action to fight against the Industrial Relations Act. If a union does act against the policy of Congress or the advice of the General Council, Congress possesses the sanction of suspension and ultimately expulsion. This threat is only used in serious cases; for example, twenty unions were expelled for registering under the Industrial Relations Act.

In 1970, a new system of industrial, committees was also set up. These are made up of members of the General Council and representatives of the main unions in the industry concerned. These committees have permitted unions to develop and coordinate industrial policies. For example, during the 1980 steelworkers dispute the TUC Steel Committee was able to negotiate directly with the British Steel Corporation. The industrial committees may represent one way in which the TUC can develop agreed industrial strategies in the future. In addition, more thoroughgoing changes to revamp TUC organization are being canvassed.

So far in this chapter, we've looked at how trade unions operate democratically in deciding on and implementing policies. But the successful implementation of these policies will depend on negotiations taking place with their members' employers. In the next chapter, we'll examine how unions win the right to negotiate on their members' behalf.

Further reading

R. Fletcher, *Trade Union Rules* (Arrow, 1979) is a good, simple account of not only what's in the rule book, but how they operate in practice in the context of union democracy. Shop-stewards' organization in the post-war period is described in C. Baker and P. Caldwell, *Unions and Change Since 1945* (Pan, 1981). If you want to read about some of the research thats been done about shop-floor organization and union branches try E. Batstone, I. Boraston and S. Frenkel, *Shop Stewards in Action* (Blackwell, 1977) or I. Boraston, H. Clegg and M. Rimmer, *Workplace and Union* (Heinemann, 1975).

Chapter Five

Getting recognition

The Woodlands Hotel is a medium sized residential hotel in Manchester. In November 1979, there was an argument between the management and workers about work rotas. As a result of this dispute, the workers saw the need for union protection. They decided to join the General and Municipal Workers' Union which organizes hotel workers. The management were not pleased by this move. They retaliated by reducing wages from £1.30 an hour to 90p an hour and increasing the workload.

This succeeded in intimidating many of the workers, particularly part timers who were new to trade unionism and unsure of their ground. They accepted the new conditions and left the union. Eleven workers stood firm and rejected the worsening of their already poor conditions. They were sacked.

The eleven workers and the union had big problems. The hotel was able to keep on functioning without their labour. They had to put on pickets outside the hotel and ask other workers such as brewery drivers not to deliver goods to the hotel. The brewery workers agreed not to cross the picket lines. However, management hired a security company and brought in food and drink in their own cars. The eleven strikers had to ask other workers to help them man the picket lines and black deliveries to the hotel.

The workers themselves were under tremendous pressures. Two of them had to continue living in the hotel where they were charged £15 a night. They had the heat and light cut off from their rooms. Another striker returned to find all her clothes and belongings dumped outside her room in a bag and had to leave the hotel.

You might find it difficult to believe that situations like this happen in this country today. Yet this is not an isolated example. It is typical of cases we have seen in the last ten years.

It shows:

● Many employers today still have the same attitudes as their forerunners a hundred years ago. They are not willing to accept that workers have a right to join a trade union and settle their terms and conditions of employment by collective bargaining.

● In many cases where workers join a union they can expect intimidation and the sack. Joining a union and getting recognition needs a lot of thought and planning if workers are to succeed in their objectives.

● In all too many cases workers will be forced into striking by an intransigent employer. The more preparation and planning workers can put into this, the more likely they are to be successful.

● In most disputes about union recognition the workers involved are not able to win the dispute by their own efforts. They have to rely to some extent on help from other unionists. The more ability workers directly involved have to mobilize support from other workers, the more successful they are going to be in getting the employer to concede recognition.

In this chapter, therefore, we attempt to give some help and guidance on some of the problems involved once you have joined a union and are attempting to achieve recognition from the employer.

We will look at:
● the extent to which recognition is still a problem;
● how you should go about organizing and recruiting;
● how you can persuade an employer that he should allow workers the basic democratic right of being represented by a union.

Attitudes of employers and the state to recognition

A hundred years ago the attitude of the average employer to trade unionism was the same as his attitude to fleas or scabies. He did his best to avoid it in the first place. Whilst it was there it was a constant irritant, and he was constantly attempting to get rid of it by every method possible. We have seen that the employers were originally supported by the state which passed laws like the Combination Acts banning trade unions. When pressure from workers forced governments to at least recognize that unions had a right to exist, the judges took over. They developed case law so that most trade union activities were made illegal. Union activities were said by the judges to be 'conspiracies' and 'in restraint of trade'. When unions took industrial action they were said to be inducing workers to break their contracts of employment. Until the last part of the nineteenth century a worker who broke his contract of employment by, say, taking a day off without permission was committing a criminal offence. The same did not apply to an employer who broke his part of the contract by sacking a worker!

Trade unions fought for the right to organize, to bargain with the employer and to take industrial action in two ways. They fought employers at the level of the enterprise and company. They also fought to make Parliament more democratic and responsive to the wishes of ordinary working people, eventually founding the Labour Party. By the early years of this century pressure had led to legislation in 1906 and 1913 which went a fair way to allowing unions to carry out their basic objectives unhindered by the law.

Similarly, a change took place in the attitudes of employers. There had always been a minority who had regarded trade unionism as a mild disability one could live with if leading an otherwise healthy life. As the trade union movement grew and increased its strength and as ordinary workers won the vote, more employers began to see the limitations of a policy of repression.

Many employers began to see the possibilities of furthering their own interests by accepting trade unions and collaborating with them. Once defeated, trade unions had an annoying habit of growing up again and constant strikes did not help profitability. If he recognized the union, the employer could defuse a focus of discontent at one go. The union provided a means by which problems could be dealt with one at a time and discussed. If there was no recognition minor problems might build up and the employer could be faced with a sudden stoppage, Trade union officials, the employers found, were often 'reasonable to deal with' and if he handled them the right way the employer could build up a good relationship with them and they could then be useful in persuading their members to accept agreed solutions. Moreover, far-sighted employers could see that certain improvements in wages and conditions could help in motivating the work-force, raising morale and increasing productivity.

More and more employers began to move away from open warfare. They increasingly saw unions as potentially helpful to the stability and security of their enterprise if their aims and goals could be moderated in the direction of responsibility. Employers were more willing to work with unions and even collaborate with them by encouraging the closed shop in highly competitive trades. Here unions could limit competition by enforcing minimum wages. Where the unions could not control all of their labour market so that there was more competition, then collaboration was less likely.

Since 1945, therefore, the orthodox view of both governments and employers has been that unions have a right to exist and to be recognized by employers for the purposes of collective bargaining. Exactly what unions should *do* with recognition, exactly what their role should be in twentieth century society, however, has been the subject of the sharpest controversy. And so employers and the state have often attempted to weaken unions' bargaining power.

Most employers have held the 'progressive' attitude we have described but by no means all. There has been a sizeable minority of employers hostile to the recognition of trade unions. In the 1960s and 1970s, employers could still be found arguing that trade unionism was unnecessary, that it led to feather bedding and restrictive practices, that trade unionism impeded progress by preventing the introduction of new technology, that it interfered with dynamic management. That whilst it was acceptable on the shop-floor, it could lead to conflicts of loyalty for managerial employees. Nor have these employers been inactive. They have firmly opposed the introduction of trade unionism into a workplace or a particular group of employees by either: new style 'benevolent suppression', increasing wages and salaries, granting fringe benefits, setting up staff associations as management fronts; or by old style 'forcible repression', victimization, sackings and blacklisting.

A recognition problem?

Most of the suggestions for and attempts at reforming industrial relations in the UK in the last fifteen years have accepted therefore that a recognition problem does exist. The Report of the Royal Commission on Trade Unions and Employers Associations, 'The Donovan Report', in 1968 pointed out that despite state support for collective bargaining since before the century:

. . . many problems of union recognition still exist. For example the Amalgamated Engineering Union was reported to have been refused recognition by seventy-two firms in the course of 1965 almost all of which employed less than 200 workers . . . The Transport and General Workers Union has reported that it has difficulty in obtaining recognition in industries where there are considerable numbers of medium- and small-sized firms. Serious difficulties have arisen in banking and in insurance.

Governments at the time of the Industrial Relations Act (1971) and the Employment Protection Act (1975) saw no need to differ from this view, and both pieces of legislation attempted to deal with this problem. If anybody doubted that there was a recognition problem the scales should have fallen from their eyes when the recognition procedure under the Employment Protection Act began to work. In 1977 before the procedure was weakened by the judges, applications from unions were being received at the rate of fifty every month.

A specimen under the microscope

When we think about workers getting organized we often have a mental picture of an overalled shop-steward standing by a machine in a factory with a spanner in his hand. However, think for a minute about the hotel and catering industry, a key element in the UK's growing tourist trade and vital to the economy. Nearly 900,000 people work in hotels, restaurants, pubs and clubs and for catering contractors like those who run your works canteen. This work-force is much bigger than that in most manufacturing industries and it is growing by about 15 per cent a year, whilst the number of workers in manufacturing is declining. Yet in this vigorous 'new' industry trade unionism is extremely weak. *The* TGWU *has under 25,000 members, the* GMWU *under 10,000.*

Why should union organization be so weak? Is it because wages are now so reasonable and working conditions so good that unions are no longer required in the 1980s? Let us look at the facts. Because of the lack of union representation minimum wages are set for all licensed hotels and restaurants by a wages council. This is a body established by the government to set rates where collective bargaining is not strong enough to do so. It consists of representatives of employers, trade unions and 'independents'. In 1977, the minima for service workers in London varied between £36 and £38. The first £6 of their tips could be deducted from a worker's wages.

A maximum of £8.40 could be deducted from wages for accommodation and £4 deducted for meals. Now this might seem bad enough but unfortunately it does not represent the true picture. When the wages inspectorate carried out an inspection in 1977, they discovered that one in eight pubs, one in five licensed restaurants, and one in three unlicensed restaurants were underpaying and were not even meeting the wage council minimum rates. Not that an employer has much to fear from discovery. The maximum fine is £100 and there are less than 150 inspectors to cover the three million workers covered by various wages councils.

Basic conditions make working in this industry an unpleasant experience. Hours are long and workers tend to work split shifts. Work is often seasonal and irregular with workers employed on a casual basis without seasonal accommodation. Living conditions for clients often contrast with those of staff.

But is it not true that wages and conditions are poor because of inefficient working, low productivity and low profits? You can judge for yourself.

- In 1977 58 per cent of males and 91 per cent of females working manually in hotels were earning under £50 per week. *This figure includes all non-cash benefits such as meals and accommodation provided by the employer.* It was about equivalent to what an average family would receive from supplementary benefit.
- In 1977 Trust House Forte made £38 million and Grand Metropolitan made £18 million in pre-tax profits. These are the two largest hotel companies. Moreover, many hotel companies like Grand Metropolitan also have extensive and lucrative holdings in other industries.

For many workers in hotels and catering wages and conditions are as bad in the 1980s as they were for workers in the last century. Moreover, there is a link between the poor conditions and the lack of union organization. More and more workers are realizing that this is the answer.

The recognition problem generally

We have looked at some particular situations but the recognition problem is unfortunately more general. Problems of union recognition can often exist where there are:

- Small scattered workplaces.
- High labour turnover.
- Workers who work in offices, particularly in private industry, and who have had little experience of unions and are sometimes hostile to them.
- A high proportion of women workers with no tradition of trade unionism.
- A high proportion of immigrant workers who may have little knowledge of trade unions. They can often be insecure, if employed on work permits, for example, and therefore open to intimidation by the employer.

Recognition problems can therefore exist across industry. However, they are particularly acute in areas where you get a concentration of the above factors.

Examples are:

Hotels and catering

Shops and distribution

Farm work

The clothing industry

Building and construction

Insurance, banking and finance

White collar workers in manufacturing industry

We can get another view of the recognition problem by looking at the figures on trade union membership. Look again at Figure 1 on page 25. In 1948 about 45 per cent of the workforce were union members, by the mid-sixties this figure had dropped to about 42 per cent. The reason for this was simple. Trade union membership had been strongest in industries such as the mines, the docks, steel and the railways. In the post war period, these industries were shedding manpower fast. Service industries were growing and within industries there was an increase in 'white collar workers'. In these areas workers were not used to unions and neither were employers. In expanding areas membership grew, but not fast enough to make up for the decline in the historical strongholds of trade unionism.

However, whilst labour force trends are still working against unions, the last ten years has been a period of rapid growth. The main increase has come from white collar workers generally and women workers particularly. It seems that many workers who in the past viewed unions with suspicion, reserve or even open hostility have changed their minds. Workers in the last decade have been faced with rampant inflation, growing unemployment and the belief that differentials were being narrowed. At the same time, they have been faced with government incomes policies. It seems that faced with this situation more and more workers have seen unions not as a problem but as an answer to these problems. They have voted with their feet and joined up despite the tremendous amount of bad publicity unions have received.

However, whilst the attitudes of many workers have changed the attitudes of many employers have not. In a research paper for the Royal Commission, Professor George Bain pointed out that even if workers decide that they want to join a union:

A major obstruction to the expansion of union membership is *employers refusal to recognize unions* and their pursuance of policies designed to discourage or prohibit their employees from joining them.

The number of strikes over recognition show that the situation is still the same today. Half of the work-force are still not in trade unions. The picture is a varied one. In some industries 95 per cent of the work-force are union members. In other industries the figure is below 10 per cent. It is in the non-union areas that workers have low earnings and insecurity of employment. They work the longest hours, face the most uncivilized discipline and are most exposed to accidents and industrial disease. Being non-union can damage your wealth and health! With no union, with no collective strength, workers have no power to control the employer.

More and more workers are realizing that this *is* the situation. More and more workers *are* putting their money where their mouth is and joining a union. However, while recognition has been a problem for workers in many industries it is particularly difficult in those industries or occupations containing a significant proportion of female or black workers.

Unions and discrimination

Bill was one of two male cleaners on a night shift. When his mate decided to leave, Bill's girl friend Pat went along one night to try the work, as the manager had said that if Bill could find somebody he would be happy working with then that person could have the job. Pat found the work suitable but it was a different story when Bill suggested to the manager that she should be taken on. He said that the work was far too strenuous for a woman and he gave the job to a man.

Abdul Karim had over two years' experience with heavy goods vehicles. He answered an advert for a heavy goods vehicle driver with a firm of haulage contractors. He discussed his qualifications and experience over the phone with Brian Jebson one of the company's directors. He was invited to take a test and asked for his name and address. When he replied, 'Abdul Karim', Mr Jebson said: 'I don't think the lads will like that'. He muttered something about insufficient experience and put down the phone.

These are two fairly mild examples of the kind of discrimination which takes place everyday against women and members of ethnic minorities in British industry. Both cases were taken to industrial tribunals where, assisted by the Equal Opportunities Commission and the Commission for Racial Equality respectively, the applicants received compensation. We would argue that the best way to deal with this kind of discrimination is through a union. The union can act at an early stage to sort the matter out:

● The union is more likely to have the confidence of the workers than an outside body.
● The union can get a worker the job he wants or get him

reinstated. By and large a tribunal is only involved with compensation.

In the past, many women and black workers have not joined unions and where they have there have been particular problems. Let us look first at women. In the past fifteen years, there has been a large increase in the number of women working. There are now about ten million women wage earners, of whom about two-thirds are married. However, women are concentrated in certain kinds of jobs. Over half of all women workers are employed in three industries: professional and scientific services which includes nursing and teaching; the distributive trades; and other service industries including the least skilled and lowest paid jobs as in catering. By and large women do 'women's job's. Where they do the same work as men they earn less. Despite the Sex Discrimination Act differentials between men and women are not narrowing:

● In 1978 women's hourly pay was on average only 72 per cent of men's hourly pay.
● In 1978 57 per cent of female manual workers and 40 per cent of female non-manual workers earned less than £50 a week. The comparative figures for men were 6 per cent of male manual workers and 4 per cent for male non-manual workers.

In the last ten years women have been joining unions at an increasing rate. In 1964 28 per cent of women were in unions. Now the figure is 37 per cent. In the last ten years the female membership of NUPE increased by 320,000 or 236 per cent; the female membership of the TGWU by 123,000 or 63 per cent; that of COHSE increased by 120,000 or 310 per cent, and that of ASTMS by 67,000, an amazing 721 per cent. Women now constitute 70 per cent of the membership of the CPSA and 66 per cent of NUPE. In the National Union of Tailor and Garment Workers women make up 90 per cent of the membership.

Where there are problems in women organizing this is not because they are women. Where women work alongside men they are just as union conscious. It is true that in the past there were problems because women only worked for brief periods and tended to have individualistic views from being at home a lot of the time. However, by and large, the problems women face in organizing and gaining recognition are the general complex of problems; low pay, high turnover, backward employers, which characterize the areas in which they work.

Despite myths about pin money, for example, recent surveys have shown that up to one in five households depend on women's earnings whilst individual women have pioneered the way into a wide range of jobs.

However, women still make up an extra exploited group and many of them remain outside unions. It is up to unions to take up more aggressively the specific problems of women and aim recruitment specifically at them. We look later on at some of the points to remember and consider where women are getting organized.

When we are talking about discrimination against ethnic minorities, we are largely talking about discrimination against blacks. There are over three-quarters of a million black workers in industry. Again black workers are largely concentrated in unskilled jobs with poor pay and conditions. Again they tend to work in certain areas such as clothing, food manufacture, metal manufacture, hotels and catering and public transport, generally in the most unskilled jobs. A detailed survey in the mid 1970s showed that in the 25–34 age group black male workers earned 85 per cent of the earnings of white male workers and in the 35–44 age group, 89 per cent of the earnings of white male workers. A recent report from the Department of Employment stated that black workers:

. . . are concentrated in conurbations where the pressure of demand for labour has usually been relatively high and in semi-skilled and unskilled jobs to which it is difficult to attract other workers because of such features as low earnings, a need to work unsocial hours and or unpleasant working conditions.

A volume of research over the past twenty-five years has also shown that black workers suffer systematic discrimination in hiring pay and conditions, promotion and dismissal from both employers and trade unionists. For example, a report by Political and Economic Planning in the late '60s found that 40 per cent of West Indian and Asian men interviewed claimed that they had been refused a job on racial grounds. Many named the employers involved, and when white and black actors were sent to apply for these jobs the firms involved did in the majority of cases discriminate. A further PEP inquiry in the middle '70s reported that an Asian or West Indian applying for an unskilled job faced discrimination in at least one third and perhaps as many as two thirds of all cases. For many years trade unions have tended to ignore the special problems which black workers have faced. The prevalent attitude was summed up by the TUC in 1964 when they reported:

. . . the General Council has no evidence that the trades unions provided special services for immigrants nor did they consider that these were necessary or desirable. (TUC Report of 1964 Congress)

In a whole series of strikes where black workers took action to stand up for their rights – the most famous were those at Mansfield Hosiery and at Imperial Typewriters – black workers received little understanding, sympathy or support from white workers or indeed from union officials.

Despite this short-sighted response the 1976 PEP report found that black workers are only too willing to join unions. At all levels from unskilled to professional they found a higher percentage joined unions than did their white counterparts. Among Asian and West Indian men 61 per cent were members of a union, compared with 48 per cent of white men. Just over one in three of Asian and West Indian women were union members, about the same proportion as white women.

Recent situations such as Grunwick suggest that, once having joined a union, black workers are willing to endure tremendous pressures and hardships in the fight for trade union recognition. Recently this position has found a response with the trade union movement in the face of the growth of the

National Front, activity by black workers and unfavourable publicity in certain strike situations. Unions have seen the need to aim specifically at black workers who are concentrated in the unorganized areas, by providing recruitment literature in minority languages, pushing for more black shop stewards and attempting to combat the racism of white workers.

There is a reservoir of black workers in poorly paid sweat shops who often appreciate the need for a union but face employer hostility. There is a need for a sustained campaign to help these workers in the face of severe organizing difficulties and employer intransigence.

Getting recognition

You should not expect automatic hostility from your employer even if he has never dealt with a union before. You may be lucky. What we have been saying is that employers demonstrate different attitudes to recognizing a union. Over most of British industry today, larger employers take a 'progressive' or 'sophisticated' attitude towards recognition. Not only are they willing to recognize a union but they see certain positive advantages in doing so. The cost of removing trade unionism in practical and political terms would be too great. Unions are there, so why not use them so that they might even become a useful adjunct to management?

Alongside these 'civilized men' of British industry, however, sit the 'fanatics', the 'hardnuts' and the 'waverers'. The fanatic is possessed of an almost religious fervour against trade unions. Inspired by the Almighty, he sees his mission in life as ensuring that they never poison the atmosphere of his enterprise. In this category would be a firm like D. C. Thomson, publishers of such literary gems as the *Beano* and *Dandy*, who have stubbornly resisted successive attempts at unionism since 1926. In many cases, the fanatic would rather close down than accept union recognition.

Whereas the fanatic does not look at a simple economic calculation of the advantages and disadvantages to him of unions, but has a mystical view of management prerogatives, the hardnut is altogether more down to earth and realistic. He does not want a union because he feels it will saddle the company with higher wages, more expensive conditions and less profits and interfere with the day to day efficient running of the company, by opening all sorts of day to day matters to joint decision with the union. The hardnut will, however, make a rational calculation when his workers strike for recognition. He will fight but if he feels the game is not worth the candle, he will concede – albeit grudgingly. He will fulminate against unions at CBI conferences until his dying day. He will never give up his fantasies of one big happy family, but at the end of the day he will do business with the union.

'The waverer' is an altogether different kettle of fish. He probably feels that unions are all right for those in overalls and flat caps, but he is rather disturbed when skilled white collar workers or managerial employees start organizing. He feels that the line has to be drawn somewhere. He is also torn between state policy supporting the extension of collective bargaining and his views on the rights of the individual. He reconciles these views by arguing that union recognition should be granted for a particular group when an 'overwhelming majority' have voted for recognition in a secret ballot. The waverer, however, will not put up much of a fight. He would, in a rather lukewarm way, prefer not to have recognition for a particular group. He feels that they should meet certain criteria first but if, for example, the Advisory, Conciliation and Arbitration Service (ACAS) says 'recognize the union', that is good enough for him. (We'll discuss the role of ACAS a little later in this chapter.)

When you are trying to come to a decision on what is the best way to go about getting recognition you need to consider which category your management falls into. For example, ACAS would be wasted on the fanatic and is not going to win for you with the hardnut, though it might add a little pressure, but can work well with the waverer.

The decision by workers in a particular workplace to join a union and set about gaining recognition can come in a variety of ways. Here are two examples.

In 1962, Fine Tubes opened a new factory in Plymouth. Local labour was quickly attracted by the fact that the employers, an American company who manufactured high quality tubing for a large range of products, was paying wages in advance of those for comparable jobs in the area. The company did not recognize trade unions. It became clear about a year after production began in late 1962 that wages elsewhere were catching up and that working conditions were deteriorating.

Dick Williams had been a card carrying union member on various other jobs. He had not been a shop-steward but had always been a strong Labour Party supporter. He had kept up his union membership and now, dissatisfied with the situation, he instinctively looked towards a union as providing a way out. He quickly found about a dozen other workers who had retained union membership and they then decided to recruit others before requesting recognition.

We came to a point where a couple of the lads were threatened by a foreman that if they were seen to be recruiting for the union they would be 'up the road', so what we had to do was approach people behind the scenes. We'd got two people in as 'collectors', one was up in the stores. That was a good place to recruit from as well because everyone had to go there some time. Anyway, this lad got called into the office by the management about trying to organize and he was threatened with the sack.

Once the management realized we were beginning to get organized they must have told the foremen that it had to be stopped. Still, we increased it until we had a membership of over thirty-five out of about eighty, so we called the officials in and told them we wanted recognition.

(From Tony Beck, *The Fine Tubes Strikes*, Stage One, 1974.)

Grunwick is a company in Brent, North London, which processes photographs. In the summer of 1976, it employed about 500 workers, largely Asian women. Throughout the summer, dissatisfaction with wages and conditions had been increasing. Tensions had been building up. For example, in one department consisting of 102 people, twenty-seven had left in July and August 1976, and nine of these had been sacked. The workers had not talked in any coherent way of joining a union but discussions had taken place. Mrs Desai, one of the leaders of the eventual strike, had discussed the poor conditions at work with her husband who worked for the Rank Organization and who told her: 'In your place if there is a union this type of management cannot behave like this towards you.' Another worker, Devshi Bhudia, had been complaining about the low wages, poor conditions, short holidays restricted to winter, and the compulsory overtime. He had suggested to some of his friends that they should join a union.

About a week after this discussion, on Friday 20 August, a group of workers including Devshi Bhudia, began a go slow in protest against the pressures management was placing on them. Devshi was sacked and three other workers walked out. That same evening, as Mrs Desai was leaving, she was involved in an argument with management as to whether or not she was leaving early. She asked for her cards and stormed out followed by her son. The six workers who had been sacked or walked out spent the weekend planning their next step. They decided to join a union, and on the Monday stood outside the factory to get a list of signatures of those willing to join with them. It was then that one of the strikers went to a Citizens Advice Bureau and asked about a trade union. He was given the telephone numbers of the TUC and Brent Trades Council. They were advised to get in touch with APEX. They were told that there was a branch meeting the following evening and it was at this meeting that the sixty or more workers who had agreed to join filled in APEX application forms. (See Jack Dromey, *Grunwick: The Workers Story*, (Lawrence & Wishart, 1978); Joe Rogaly, *Grunwick*, (Penguin, 1978).)

These two cases illustrate the two ends of the spectrum. In the first case, initially one worker tapped the tradition of trade unionism he had grown up with when faced with difficulties in a non-union workplace. Having found others in a similar position, they then started a careful recruiting campaign before showing their hand. Not surprisingly, management soon discovered what was going on. However, at this stage they either did not see the union as a major threat or, for particular reasons, they did not want a strike at this particular time. They threatened, but did not take decisive action such as sacking members. Enough time had been bought to build up a base sufficient for the workers to show their hand and call in the officials.

This will be more typical and preferable to the second case. Rather than a planned strategy what we had here was an explosion. There was a slow accumulation of grievances but no channel for solving them. Because none of the workers were in touch with a union, neither was there a tactical sitting on grievances whilst using their build-up and resultant bad feeling to recruit workers. In the Fine Tubes case, workers with union experience in the past always saw the union as a concrete answer to their problems but they saw the need to plan and build carefully. In the Grunwick case we are dealing with immigrant workers with cultural barriers and little tradition of unionism. Only a few of the workers saw the union as an answer, and then as a vague aspiration. It took the eruption of 20 August when they ended up on the outside to focus matters and jolt them into seeking out a union. Understandably, compared with the Fine Tubes example, the behaviour of the workers here was off the cuff and unplanned.

Unions in this country are not renowned for the vigour or success of their recruitment drives. The impulse to union membership and recognition will generally come from within a workplace. However, there are examples of union officials making contact with those inside what they regard as an important workplace; of stewards from the shop-floor stimulating unionism in the office; of workers in one plant of a company setting out to unionize other plants; and of unions sending dedicated missionaries to convert the unbelievers in non-union establishments. Union recognition situations have also occurred:

● Where employees have become dissatisfied with a staff association fostered and dominated by an employer and have decided that they would prefer real trade unionism.
● Where there has been no, or minimal, union membership

and the employer has had his own system for periodically adjusting wages and conditions. Dissatisfaction had been slowly building up and a particular settlement precipitates wholesale union recruitment.

● Where a union has taken to arbitration a non-union firm where it has some membership under one of the laws on extension of terms and conditions of employment and the resultant award has led to a bargaining relationship.

By and large recruitment and recognition are more successfully achieved with a lot of planning and preparation. When an 'explosion' occurs or when an employer precipitates action you are in a better position to react. Your planning and turning may be upset if members spontaneously walk out over a particular problem. But if you already have the rudiments of organization laid down then you are in a better position to turn this into a general recognition dispute. Situations like Grunwick, where workers join and organize afterwards are rare. Here are some basic points to remember if you are trying to organize the union in your workplace.

Winning the arguments

You yourself may be convinced as to the advantages of union membership. You may be convinced that union membership is good for the work-force. However, you may accept this as something you have always believed in and not thought about too much. You have to think through the arguments for joining a union clearly, so that you can use them with other workers. If you know your workmates well you will know which arguments to give most weight to with each individual. You should also be familiar with the type of arguments used against trade unions (see Chapter two).

You should be ready with answers prepared when workers say: 'Aren't trade unions killing patients in hospitals by going on strike?' 'Isn't Moss Evans just like our boss here in the company. Why should I pay so that I can have two bosses ordering me about?' 'Where does my money go in actual fact if I join the union?' and 'Won't I get wage increases negotiated by the union anyway even if I don't join?'

Remember that your workmates will probably get their view of what unions are doing from the selective and sensational coverage in papers such as the *Sun* and *Mirror*. If you read a paper like the *Financial Times* you might be able to find out what some of the disputes that catch the headlines are actually about and why unions take up certain positions.

You should always try and talk to workers when they are new to the company, particularly those with union experience. After they have become settled it may be difficult to get them to break routine by joining a union. Are there any workplaces near your work that you can use to show that unions can do a good job, particularly in firms in your own industry, close competitors, subsidiaries or other establishments of your employer? Practical examples may convince workers or you may be able to introduce them to shop-stewards from elsewhere.

Always have copies of the union journal which publicizes union achievements and always have available union literature which may help you with arguments.

Organization and issues

There is always a need to go slowly and carefully when trying to organize a union. There is no time for self-indulgence or mock heroics. There will be times where you have to bite your tongue, accept an injustice and avoid a provocation from management which is intended to get you to show your hand too quickly. Where the employer is very hostile, you may have to carry out recruitment in secret.

If you are in a fair-sized workplace try to get a reliable member in each department. These members can then be made responsible for recruiting in their department and you can hold regular meetings with them to discuss progress. At the start these meetings can be informal and in the face of employer hostility are best held off the premises and outside working hours. You will always have a problem in negotiating or in a dispute if your members are concentrated in only one or a few areas of the workplace. You must try and spread union membership and involvement as widely as possible.

You will find it easier to recruit once a sizeable group have joined. You often get a snowballing effect. Particularly important is to look for key groups of workers, the groups that management most relies upon. These may be the most skilled workers or those at the start of the production process or specialized groups like drivers. If you can build in these areas, then you are building your bargaining power and also setting an example to the weaker groups. Workers may join for a variety of reasons – sometimes even because others whom they respect or like have joined.

We have pointed out that whilst you may win some workers to the union through debate and discussion, you will find that argument works best where workers think they are faced with a practical problem. You should draw up a mental map of the problems in the workplace:

● What are the issues that bother workers in each department or section?
● What do workers want that they have not got?
● What conditions need improving?
● What are the most important grievances?
● What are the problems that affect most workers and can provide the possibility of united action?

If all workers on the same rates and wages are poor then money may be the obvious issue. On the other hand, if workers are on piece-rates or doing different jobs the conditions in which you work may be more central. Many recognition disputes have occurred where management has wanted to introduce changes in work patterns or the production process. The discussion this has involved has focussed light on work as a whole and has often brought underlying discontent dramatically to the surface.

The timing of a recognition claim is important but sometimes difficult to control. Again, planning is probably best. Here you are drawing attention to problems and grievances, stockpiling them as future ammunition and using them as part of the recruitment process. When you are strong enough, or where your strength coincides with a major issue coming up, you approach management. On the other hand, remember that you do have to keep the time scale reasonably short. We are talking of months not years. Too prolonged a period of waiting can lead to demoralization and loss of membership. The other type of situation is one where the volcano erupts and your members are quickly demanding a walk out. Careful planning is preferable because you can pick your time. If you work in a hotel you are negotiating from a strong position at tourist peaks; if you work in a big shop the employer may be more willing to listen to you in December at the peak of Christmas shopping. Miners, for example, do not strike in summer! If you are able to pick your time then this will depend on factors such as the state of the employer's order book, his present profitability and plans for work changes, new investment or introduction of new machinery and his future projections. This means you will need to know as much as you possibly can about your employer (see later in this chapter for details of how to do this). What will also be vitally important here will be the morale and attitude of your members at the particular time.

However, you may be faced seven times out of ten with either the explosive outburst or the situation we looked at earlier in which the employer seizes the initiative. We will look at the best way to deal with this later on. At the right moment do not go in and just say, 'we want recognition', put something concrete on the table. Go in when there is a major issue you can use. If you come out and say, 'We've got recognition,' the members may murmur, 'We'll get pie in the sky when we die.' Ask for a wage increase, shorter hours, more holidays, better sickness benefit, better safety measures. Whatever 'fits' at that point in time, but always try to get: more money; an agreement to establish grievance and disciplinary procedures; and an agreement to allow facilities and time-off for shop-stewards. (We'll take up the details of these issues in another chapter.)

In other words you must get the organization off the ground and also put something in your members' pockets. This will illustrate that the union *can* do something, can bring home the bacon. It will show that all your talking *was* on the right lines. This will strengthen the support of existing members and help attract new members to the union.

During the build-up period you should maintain the closest links with your union organization outside work. As we have stressed earlier, attend branch meetings and make contacts; be in close touch with your branch secretary and full-time officers. Let them know regularly in detail exactly what progress you are making, so that they will be ready and have some idea of the picture if you call for help. Always listen to their advice and recommendations. They will often speak from wide experience. But remember that this experience must be blended with your own on the spot assessment. You should also be in contact with trade unionists in other parts of your company. You may need their support if difficulties occur. Find out about your employers, customers and suppliers. For example, if your employer gets crucial components for his work from a supplier which is strongly unionized, then you may be able to persuade the union members there not to deliver the components to your employer. In most recognition disputes, this kind of blacking is vital.

How to find out about your company

Any workplace union organization should try and become, over a time, a data bank of information about the employer. This can help you to:

- build links with other workers employed by your employer to your mutual advantage;
- build up knowledge of the employer's prospects, strengths and weaknesses;
- generate financial information useful to you in collective bargaining.

Suppose you only vaguely know that Engels, Ermen and Co. is just one of many businesses, all owned by some larger company – perhaps a foreign company. How can you find out who owns your company, what other firms the same

119

group owns and how your particular organization fits into the larger picture?

First, find out if your company is a private or public one. (A public company is one which is owned by shareholders who purchase their shares on a stock exchange.) A book which will help you here is *Who Owns Whom*, published annually. This should be available in any major library. One volume lists all UK public companies, some major private ones, major US firms in Britain and their subsidiaries. The other lists subsidiaries and names the owning firm.

Next, you will want to find out how much wealth your company creates – and how that wealth is divided up between workers who produce it and the owners of the firm. This is not the same as asking about the firm's 'profits'. There is much talk about 'profits and losses' for firms, but in fact there are so many ways of calculating profits that the term cannot be trusted. Your company, with the help of your mates, produces goods or services that someone buys. (If you are in a public service, such as NHS, the government in effect buys your service.) So something of value is created and exchanged for money. In order to find out how much value you and your fellow workers created and how it was divided up, you must analyse the company's financial accounts.

If your firm is a public firm it is required by law to publish several important sets of figures. Usually the firm will do this in an *Annual Report* for shareholders. These financial accounts include: The profit and loss statement, the source and application of funds statement, and the balance sheet, along with detailed notes to the accounts which often contain more useful information than the statements themselves. Once you know what to look for in the published accounts you can answer such questions as:

● How much wealth has our firm created in the past year?
● How was the firm's income divided up between the workers and the owners?
● Where did the firm get its funds from and how did it spend them?

- How much investment has the firm made in new plant and equipment?
- How valid is management's claim of poverty?
- How much are the directors paying themselves?

The major reasons why trade unionists need to understand the firm's financial position are, of course, so they can press for a fairer share of the wealth that is created and so that they can see what the prospects are for future employment in the firm, i.e. wages and job security. If you have difficulty getting copies of the firm's published financial reports, most major libraries will have copies, as well as Extel Cards published by Extel Statistical Services. These summarise certain companies' published reports over a number of years and also list subsidiaries, directors, major activities, etc. In addition, the information required by government is filed in Companies House, 55 City Road, London EC1. This applies to both public and private firms. If you are an affiliate of the Labour Research Department, 78 Blackfriars Road, London SE1, you can also ask them for information about a firm and your own union's research department may help you.

A word of caution – beware of financial reports prepared especially for trade unionists. They often 'simplify' to the point of falsifying information.

These accounts are, in any case, for the past year or years. When you want to know about future prospects for employment or likely funds for wage increases in the next year, you need to see the firm's cash budgets. These do not have to be published and therefore you will have to get them through collective bargaining. In addition, if you work for a multi-plant, multi-national firm with many subsidiaries, it may be difficult to get the kind of information you need for your particular part of the operation. In the end this information will have to be attained through negotiation of information agreements. In the meantime, be sceptical when the firm says it does not have information about sales, costs, profits, investment and employment plans for individual plants or operations. Without such data the firm can hardly be run efficiently – they just choose not to let you have it.

For a trade unionist trying to understand the financial position of the firm – and in some cases the parent company – it is an uphill battle. *Remember* – never rest your case only on your employer's ability to pay. What is crucial is the cost of living – *your* ability to pay.

Further reading

There are several books on particular recognition disputes, for example, T. Beck, *The Fine Tubes Strike* (Stage 1, 1974), J. Arnison, *The Million Pound Strike* (Lawrence and Wishart), J. Dromey, *Grunwick, the Workers' Story* (Lawrence and Wishart, 1978). The general issues of recognition from a trade union angle are discussed in J. McIlroy, 'Trade Union Recognition: The Limits of the Law' (WEA Studies for Trade Unionists). The practical problems facing women workers are examined in C. Aldred, *Women at Work* (Pan, 1981). A more academic account about racism in industry is given in M. Rimmer, *Race and Industrial Conflict* (Heinemann).

Chapter **Six**

Building your organization, defending your rights

In this chapter, we'll look at ways in which you can develop and extend the influence of your trade union organization. First, we'll consider ways in which your organization can be improved – looking at the closed shop, shop-stewards' rights and facilities, shop-stewards' and combine committees, and links with Constituency Labour Parties. Next we'll go on to look at the different kinds of collective agreements which can be used to further the interests of trade union members in the workplace. Lastly, we examine the organizational problems created for trade unions by the growth of unemployment.

Organizing

100 per cent membership

We have discussed the importance of 100 per cent membership in increasing your bargaining power (see page 40). You should first of all aim to achieve this objective by *persuasion*. All union members should talk to newcomers to the workplace about the advantages of union membership, about what the union has done, and ask them to join. Don't do this immediately, before the newcomer has had time to take their coat off! But it *is* useful to introduce the subject soon after a worker has started, when they are still open-minded and not settled in their ways.

The best way is to introduce the subject naturally, while describing other aspects of the job. Some newcomers will have been in unions before and will expect to join. Others will accept the union as they accept other aspects of workplace life. If you encounter problems, make sure that you have the arguments for joining the union ready (see Chapters one and two). If there are difficulties, let the shop-steward know so that he can handle the situation. Do this naturally, so that it doesn't look as if you're passing the newcomer over to the Special Branch!

In the better organized workplaces, stewards should be able to talk to newcomers as part of the interview process before the person is employed. If this is not possible, stewards should at least be given lists of new employees. However, it is the responsibility of all union members to talk to new starters, to try and recruit them to the union, and to let the steward know of their presence in the workplace. Newcomers will sometimes be impressed by the enthusiasm of a rank and file member who works closely with them. They may see the steward initially as a remote stranger.

With a reluctant worker, avoid the heavy-handed approach. Be patient and try to convince them. Don't give up, but don't nag them. Sooner or later they will have a practical problem at work. What seemed very vague when you were trying to convince them months before may seem very concrete now. When we're in trouble we all want to talk to someone about it and get advice. They may see now that that's where the union can help. However, you should explain to this type of worker that they must join the union first. If members and stewards solve the problems of non-members, then they don't really have any reason for joining, and existing members will ask, 'What are we paying our dues for?'

It's also important to ensure that all existing members stay in the union and are up to date with their dues. Otherwise this can affect their rights to union benefits. If collecting dues is a problem, then the union can consider negotiating a 'check-off' system. This means that the employer will deduct union dues before he pays the work-force their wages. Some employers will do this gratis; other charge a small percentage to cover the administration costs. You have to balance the ease and efficiency of this system against the loss of contact it may involve and that in physically handing over money workers think about what the union means. However, these problems can be overcome by shop-stewards making extra efforts to keep in touch with their members. Check-off frees a collector to deal with more important union business. The pros and cons of the system should be discussed by all members and their agreement given before it is introduced.

In workplaces where a substantial proportion of the employees are union members, it may be decided to negotiate a 100 per cent membership agreement requiring workers to join the relevant union. This is sometimes called a union membership agreement. The advantage of this is that you increase your bargaining power and have to spend less time on recruitment since employees automatically have to become members. You can devote your energies to winning other union objectives. The danger is that you don't. Because membership is automatic, there may be a loss of interest in the union. But this isn't an insuperable problem, and the closed shop is an essential union objective. If the union meets your employer to discuss a membership agreement, one of the points he will probably raise is the legal position on closed shops.

What does the law say? If you have a closed shop and workers refuse to become, or to remain, members, then, in the end, trade unionists would argue, they will have to be sacked. The Employment Act 1980 says that such a worker will be entitled to take the employer to an industrial tribunal and get compensation. Trade unionists could also be involved if they pressurized the employer to dismiss the worker, and if the employer asks for them to be involved in the case.

If you do not have a closed shop already, then your employer will only be protected against any future legal case if you have an approved close shop. To get an approved closed shop, there has to be a secret ballot of all those to be covered by the agreement. If 80 per cent of those entitled to vote, vote in favour, then there is an approved closed shop. But if anybody who was entitled to vote in this ballot refused to join the union and was sacked as a result, then they would have a legal claim for unfair dismissal. Any new worker who refused to join or later decided to leave the union would have a similar legal claim if they were dismissed *and* if they could show that they objected to the union on grounds of conscience or other genuine personal conviction. This is very wide and might cover workers who objected to a union policy of supporting the Labour Party or nuclear disarmament.

The Government code of practice on the closed shop states that 80 per cent is a minimum figure, that employers should ask for a higher percentage, and they should also demand a very high proportion of membership before agreeing to hold any ballot. You should be able to see that this procedure is both undemocratic and unworkable for a number of reasons:

● An 80 per cent minimum of those *eligible* to vote is extremely high and you are not likely to get it. (After all, most governments are elected to power on a far lower percentage!)

● Even if you do, those who voted against are not bound by the result.

If you already have a closed shop, then existing members can opt out and newcomers can refuse to join on 'conscience' grounds. The code of practice also suggests that you have periodic reviews with an 80 per cent majority before you can continue with the closed shop.

What to do Decide after detailed discussion among union members whether the union is in a position to negotiate a closed shop. All members should understand what this implies. Decide who the agreement should cover. Ideally it will cover all existing workers and newcomers. Sometimes unions have agreed that only workers who start after a certain date must join, the assumption being that existing non-members will eventually leave or die off! Keep any exemptions as limited as possible. Conscience clauses are so wide anybody can wriggle out. Do you want to exempt religious objectors? If so, what procedure will be followed for deciding who falls within that category? Will they be required to pay the equivalent of the union dues to a charity? Is a special procedure needed to deal with those refusing to accept a closed shop agreement?

Inform management that the union isn't interested in an approved closed shop. You simply want a 100 per cent agreement and you expect management to ensure that all workers join. If they complain about legal action, the union can point out that if workers see union membership as 'going with the job' and are aware that management will not tolerate non-members, then such action is unlikely. After all, in the present high unemployment situation, who is going to risk losing a job and be put to the time and expense of representing themselves at an industrial tribunal, where even if they win their case they will only receive a relatively small sum of compensation? However, there is no doubt that the law *does* make it more difficult to negotiate a closed shop. At the least, it means your employer may be looking for some concessions from the union in return. If you already have a closed shop, insist that the status quo remains. No reviews or ballots should take place. They don't help at all.

Remember, the best kind of closed shop agreement covers everybody. Here is a simple example:

The company recognizes the union as sole representative of hourly paid workers. All such workers will join the union within their period of induction.

Members and stewards – rights and protections

Not only is 100 per cent membership important for a healthy workplace organization – so is an effective network of shop-stewards and safety representatives. You need to ask yourself: are all areas and types of job in the workplace adequately represented? Are different shifts adequately represented? Are there too many members per shop-steward? Do you need separate safety representatives or should the shop-steward do the job? (Your union may have a policy on this.) Are there regular elections for shop-steward? Make sure that management has no veto over who the shop-steward is. (After all, Bob Paisley only picks the Liverpool team, not the other side as well, whatever you might think at times!)

Before shop-stewards can be effective, they need freedom to move around the workplace, time off from their job with guaranteed earnings, and certain basic facilities. In the past, this often caused problems. Today it is dealt with by section 27 of the Employment Protection (Consolidation) Act. This gives a legal right to shop-stewards and safety representatives whose union is recognized to take time off with pay during working hours when they are dealing with matters which affect the union and their employer. Stewards should be allowed time off:

● to interview members;
● to meet management;
● to inform members about negotiations with management;
● to meet other stewards and full-time officials;

- to appear on behalf of members before outside bodies such as industrial tribunals;
- to explain to new members the role of the union in the workplace.

A code of practice 'Time Off For Trade Union Duties and Activities', produced by ACAS, the official Advisory, Conciliation and Arbitration Service, explains what these entitlements are in more detail.

The right to time off also applies to business which affects the steward's employer or an associated employer. For example, a steward would be entitled to time off to meet with stewards from other parts of his employers' group of companies or from other Area Health Authorities in the NHS. The law and the code of practice say that a steward is entitled to 'reasonable' time off. What you think is reasonable, your employer may think is excessive. Stewards should aim for what the needs of their members dictate, not what management feels that productivity requires. If there is a difference over this, negotiations will have to take place about it. Stewards must be paid their normal earnings when they take time off; they shouldn't lose any money.

The code of practice is also vague about what facilities stewards should be entitled to – they should be given '. . . the facilities necessary for them to perform their duties efficiently and to communicate effectively with members'. The code suggests that managements should provide accommodation for meetings, access to a telephone, noticeboards and, where there is a lot of union work, an office.

Finally, stewards are entitled to time off for training which is related to the type of problems that they have to deal with. Such courses must be approved by the TUC or the stewards' union. All stewards are entitled to attend the ten day courses run by the TUC in conjunction with universities, the Workers' Educational Association and further education colleges. Individual unions will also give you information on the courses that they provide for representatives. You should note that this right to time off for training is a separate right, in addition to time off for union duties.

Safety representatives are given particular rights in the Safety Representative and Safety Committee Regulations, made under the Health and Safety at Work Act, to investigate potential hazards at work, to take up members complaints about safety, and to regularly inspect the workplace. These regulations and a special code of practice give safety representatives similar rights to time off as stewards. Union members who do both jobs should make sure that they get the two bites at the cherry which they are legally entitled to. (This subject is dealt with in more detail in another book in this series, *Health and Safety at Work* by D. Eva and R. Oswald.)

The law also gives a right to stewards and ordinary members to take time off for wider union activities such as attending annual conference or district or divisional committees. The employer has to allow 'reasonable' time off here, but he is not legally required to pay the workers involved. The idea is that these activities do not have the same direct relationship to the employer as, say, a workplace negotiating meeting.

If union members are refused any of these rights, then they can take the company to an industrial tribunal within three months of the incident. However, a tribunal cannot order an employer to allow time off. It can only award compensation each occasion time off is refused or not paid for. The TUC therefore suggests:

The best method of securing satisfactory rights to time off is through the negotiation of agreements.

Such agreements should not give employers a say on representatives qualifications or size of constituency. They should provide for paid time off for both representatives and members. They should be based on the fact that the list of duties in the code of practice is not exhaustive and workers may require time off for other duties. Moreover, they should also take account of the fact that the need for time off may increase over time and requires flexibility. Fixed figures in hours per week or per year should therefore be avoided, as should strict detailed rules. Go instead for an agreement that specifies the kind of function and training for which time off is

required and which provides a simple procedure for inform-
ing management.

Protections All good trade unionists are at times liable to
be sticking their necks out. Standing up for your rights may
mean conflict with your employer. When management
attempts to discipline workers for defending union rights or
taking part in union activities, we talk of *victimization*. Consider the following examples:

The grievance procedure said that before Jack Kilroy, the staff rep.,
left his office to talk to members elsewhere he must ask his supervisors permission. Over the years Jack had extended his rights so
that by custom and practice he came and went as union business
required. One day a new supervisor asked him where he was going
and when he said 'union business' told him to return to work. Jack
went off anyway and was sacked for unauthorized absence from
work.

Del was a steward who was too fond of a drink and the sound of
his own voice. One day as he came back from the pub late he
pocketed a watch one of his members had left in the wash room.
Del was found out and sacked.

The first case is one of victimization. Jack may have been
committing a technical disciplinary offence and caution might
have been the better part of valour, but he was acting on
union business. The second case is a straightforward disciplinary matter. Del was a fool to himself and to his members.

Management may pick on trade unionists because they feel
that the union is becoming too effective or because they want
to discourage other workers from becoming involved in
union activity. This will be particularly true when the union
is first getting organized. It is against the law for your employer to sack you either for saying that you want to join a
union, or for joining a union, or for taking part in union
activities at an appropriate time. An 'appropriate time' means
a time outside working hours, for example during the lunch
hour or tea break, before or after work, or during working
hours *if* the employer has agreed. It is also against the law
for your employer to take action short of dismissal, for ex-

ample, refusing you promotion or overtime, to prevent or deter you from being a union member or from taking part in union activities at an appropriate time.

In one case, workers joined a union and asked the employer for recognition. He called a meeting of all the employees and said 'I will close the factory rather than recognize the union.' The workers took him to a tribunal where they were awarded compensation as his speech was an action intended to prevent workers joining the union. In another case, a woman who was trying to recruit new members was sacked when she left work for seven minutes to phone the union office from a call box because the employer had refused to let her use the office phone. A tribunal found that the reason for dismissal was not absence from work but union activities. However, in other cases, tribunals have taken a more restrictive view of what union activities are. Victimization is often difficult to prove. Some employers are more subtle than those described here and will disguise it as dismissal for redundancy or disciplinary reasons. Because of this problem, the ACAS code of practice on 'Disciplinary Practice and Procedures in Employment' states that in the case of lay officials 'no disciplinary action beyond an oral warning should be taken until the circumstances of the case have been discussed with a senior trade union representative or full-time official'.

If you are going to make a claim of unfair dismissal for trade union activities, you can also claim what is known as 'interim relief'. There is a special tribunal procedure for this. You must apply within seven days of the dismissal with a written statement from a full-time official saying that you are a union member and that he feels that you were dismissed for union activities. The tribunal will then meet quickly. If it feels that the full tribunal hearing which will be held later is likely to find that the official is correct, then it will order your employer to pay your wages until the full hearing.

However, there is no legal protection at all if a worker is refused a job because of past union activities, if employers operate a blacklist against known union activists. You only have rights once you are an employee.

Always remember too, that industrial tribunals can only recommend reinstatement. They cannot force an employer to take a dismissed worker back. If a worker is victimized, then it is essential that they are defended by the union. Otherwise, nobody else will be prepared to stick their neck out and the organization will suffer. The full weight of the union must be thrown into the fight against victimization. Industrial tribunals are an unreliable defence and should only be used as a last resort. Industrial action is the best way of ensuring that victimization is not successful.

Shop-stewards' committees

The next stage of organization is weaving the workplace representatives into a coordinated team (like Liverpool FC!) rather than a collection of disconnected individuals. It's important to realize that what happens in one area of the workplace affects workers in another area. A precedent set in one disciplinary case can be used against workers elsewhere. The experience and knowledge of one group can be used to help everybody. The employers have an organization in the workplace – directors, managers, supervisors, foremen, personnel officers. They have a coordinated system in which policy decisions are made and handed down; information flows down from the board to the foreman and ultimately back up again. To deal with this, trade unionists need an organization too – the shop-steward committee system. If each department or section goes its own way, management will be only too happy; they can divide and rule, and pick you off one by one. But if all the shop-stewards meet regularly, then the trade unions can present a united front.

If you work in a small workplace where everybody is in the same union, there is not too much of a problem. All the stewards should form and regularly attend a shop-stewards' committee. (If you have a workplace branch then the branch committee may take on this function). The committee should hear reports from each section, and the stewards should regularly report back to their members. It is vital that the membership know what the committee is doing. One method

133

that can be used is to produce a workplace bulletin detailing the committees activities and decisions and to which members can contribute. Keep articles short, relevant, topical and, if possible, humorous. The bulletins reproduced on pages 135 and 136 give two examples. The first concerns the threat of redundancy. The second is an extract from a bulletin on health and safety.

The job of the committee is to develop and implement a strategy for the workplace as a whole. You need to make sure that all sections are adequately represented and that there is a cross-section of technical expertise. It is important to stress again the magic ingredient: *teamwork*. Nobody can be a perfect shop-steward with a detailed grasp of the union rulebook, agreements, health and safety, job evaluation, employment law, social security benefits and occupational pension schemes. However, a committee *can* contain this expertise within its collective ranks. Make one or two members responsible for becoming an expert in each area. This is not to say that each steward should not strive to know as much as possible about all these areas, but in practice there may need to be some division of labour. Try to get stewards on different training courses dealing with their specialist area. Try and build up a stewards' library of relevant acts of Parliament, codes of practice, health and safety regulations as well as books on trade unionism and the specialist areas. The following publications will all be useful; they tell you about agreements in other areas and industries, legal matters, pensions and health and safety.

IDS *Reports, Studies* and *Briefs*, twice monthly, from Incomes Data Services, 140 Great Portland St, London W1.

Industrial Relations Review and Report, Legal Information Bulletin, Pay and Benefits Bulletin, Health and Safety Bulletin, all available from Industrial Relations Services, 67 Maygrove Road, London NW6.

These are all expensive. For example the *Pay and Benefits Bulletin* costs £45 per year. Therefore most shop-stewards' committees and branches will probably have to rely on *Labour Research* and *Bargaining Report* available from LRD Publica-

Liverpool City Council Shop Stewards & Staff Representatives Committee

DEFEND OUR JOBS
DEFEND OUR PUBLIC SERVICES

**To: All Workers and Staff Employed by Liverpool City Council
From: Liverpool City Council Shop Stewards & Staff Representatives Committee**

The LCCSS & SR Committee is a recently formed rank and file body, comprising stewards from many City Council departments. The committee came into being as a direct result of the concern felt by many employees of the various City Council departments over threats to our jobs and living standards. This concern was compounded by the advent of a government intent on destroying council jobs and public services.

The present Tory Government is threatening massive public spending cuts. For many thousands of Council workers this will mean the SACK. For millions of people it will mean reduced or non-existent services.

There is no doubt that the cuts announced have yet to make their impact, although in Liverpool the axe is already being sharpened. Closures of Old People's Homes (Croxteth Lodge); Young Persons' Homes (Sparrow Hall); Myrtle Street Children's Hospital; proposed cuts in cleansing vehicles and night watchmen are just an indication of what is on the way.

The scale of the threatened attacks promises to be unique in its impact and effect. Our response to these attacks must be equally strong, equally effective and equally unique. We feel that the most effective manner to deal with these threats to our jobs and living standards is for the workforce of the City Council to present a united front against such attacks. In the past, it has been all too easy for governments and councils to attack individual groups of workers, who, in their isolation, have been unable to effectively defend themselves. Through the LCCSS & SR Committee we are no longer isolated groups of workers, but are capable of acting in unison in defence of our jobs.

The committee has been meeting monthly since July and its importance has already been recognised by City Council leaders who met a deputation on 7th August 1979. Council leaders were left in no doubt as to the reaction of the workforce in the face of any redundancies or reduction in living standards.

The committee, at its last meeting on 20th October, called for a half day stoppage of work and mass support for a lobby of Liverpool City Council on November 7th against public spending cuts. We urge you to show your strength by supporting the lobby.

Make sure your department is represented at our next meeting – 17th November at the YMCA, Mount Pleasant. (10.00 a.m.)

It is a matter of utmost priority that we are seen to be closing our ranks against the coming attacks. Our greatest weakness lies in our seeing ourselves as small isolated units and allowing ourselves to be picked off one by one. Our greatest strength lies in our unity and with that unity we will be able to show that the price of our jobs will be a heavy one.

**Join the Committee   Elect your Delegates
Support the November 7th Stoppage and lobby of Liverpool City Council**

A Chemical Problem: Loctite Glue

Workers at Chrysler, Jaguar and now Masseys have reported problems arising from the use of Loctite glue.

Two shop-stewards at Banner Lane have raised the issue following a case of dermatitis on a worker using it.

Investigations through scientists attached to CHASM (Coventry Health and Safety Movement) have revealed:

a. That some containers now admit it can cause dermatitis (they didn't use to).
b. That it can cause nausea and loss of appetite.
c. That there is the possibility of it being a carcinogen (cause of cancer). This is not known for certain because not enough research has been done.
d. That it is a "moderately acute systemic poison".

Under sections 2 and 6 of the Health and Safety at Work Act, the stewards concerned are entitled to the full information concerning this glue. They are currently seeking to obtain this information.

Your Safety Committee Reps would like to hear of any other areas using Loctite or similar glues or any past problems. Please inform your foreman at once and see your Safety Committee Rep.

Further information is in the CHASM Checklist No. 2 on Chemicals

Extract from Massey-Ferguson Safety Representatives' Bulletin

tions, 78 Blackfriars Rd, London SE1. Also useful on safety is *Hazards Bulletin* available monthly from BSSRS, 9 Poland St, London W1V 3DG. Back copies of your union journal and the *Financial Times* will also be very useful to keep in your library.

There will need to be a basic procedure for running committee meetings (see page 159) and basic rules on policy. For example, each shop-steward has the right to argue the views of his members at the committee; he should then accept the collective decision, explain it honestly to his members and abide by it in dealings with management.

If there is more than one union in a workplace, you should form a *joint shop-stewards' committee* (JSSC). The principle here is the same – you have more in common with members of other unions than you have with the employer and you need to organize on this basis to prevent him exploiting inter-union differences. The main difference is that a joint committee will have to coordinate the bargaining strategies and reconcile the policies of different unions.

In a small workplace, all stewards can be members of the JSSC. In a larger set up, membership may need to be limited to an agreed number of stewards from each union to stop the committee becoming unwieldy. This should be supplemented by regular meetings of all stewards. Again, it's important to ensure that each group of workers is adequately represented, otherwise some may not be prepared to accept the committee's decisions. You need to think carefully about the constitution of a JSSC. What decision-making powers will the committee have? What relationship will these have to the policies of individual unions? Particular strains have been placed on some JSSCs in recent years when they have attempted to get united action, for example against government pay policies, only to find that some stewards and members have been encouraged by their unions not to participate. Another problem is to contain conflicts created by differential wages and conditions between different groups of workers. A third problem has been ensuring the presence of white collar office representatives on such committees. It often proves difficult to break down the tradition of mutual suspicion. But its important to try. It's no use manual workers complaining, as they often do, that office staff don't support them, if they've never been invited to meetings.

In a large workplace with a lot of union business, you may need stewards who spend their whole time on union duties. There may be one or more full-time stewards for each union, known as senior steward or convenor. The functions of the JSSC can often be split with the senior steward of one union acting as the works convenor and secretary of the JSSC and the senior steward of another union acting as the chairman. This can help to overcome the sectional strains which may exist between different unions.

The job of the workplace organization is to exchange information, hammer out strategy and coordinate action. This involves knowing as much about your employer as he knows about himself. We have discussed some ways in which you can dig out this information on page 119. You will very often find that to build a strong workplace organization you must organize *outside* your workplace. For example:

● the Metal Box Company has plants in twenty different countries;
● in 1970 the top one hundred manufacturing firms in the UK each had seventy-five different plants on average;
● GEC control about a hundred and fifty major companies.

Your own individual workplace is often just a pawn in a very big game. Decisions can be taken thousands of miles away which will influence the lives of you and your fellow members. Your own management may have very limited decision-making powers. This has important implications for workers' organizations:

● If you have links with workers in other parts of your company, you can build up a composite picture of what your company is up to, how it operates, what its future product and manpower strategies are likely to be.
● You can coordinate a company or multi-company union response to avoid any dangerous consequences these strategies may have for your members.

● You can adjust the bargaining imbalance by united action. Isolated workers in one plant which is shut down have little chance of winning a redundancy struggle. Their chances are improved tremendously if workers in another vital or profitable section are willing to support them.

Committees of representatives from different workplaces are called *combine committees*. They have never been more vital than today when the limitations of sectional action to prevent mass redundancy or control new technology are all too apparent. A working party of the Tyne Conference of Shop-Stewards published a practical guide on how to go about setting up a combine committee. They suggested the following points:

● identify your *real* employer;
● find out where all your employer's plants are;
● establish what kind of policies your employer is pursuing;
● make contact with employees in other plants;
● work out the details of the organization, constitutional powers and functions of the committee, as well as its financing and possible publishing activities, for example, of a combine newspaper.

All this is easier said than done. Management won't help you, and often union officials regard combine committees as a threat to the formal union structure, though this is less so now than in the past. However, this kind of joint organization is essential. You can try to fight a multinational company or a state-backed nationalized industry on a plant by plant basis – but you won't last more than a round or two.

Finally, workers are also beginning to experiment with other forms of organization. In Liverpool, shop-stewards in the TGWU have set up a coordinating committee on a geographical basis, not on the basis of common employer. This is an important development which recognizes that trade unionists are all in the same boat whoever their employer. In some multinationals, workers are attempting to build links and coordinate strategy with fellow employees of the same company in other countries, recognizing that they have more in common with workers abroad than they have with their British bosses.

Using the Labour Party

If your union is affiliated nationally to the Labour Party then your branch will be eligible for affiliation to Constituency Labour Parties. The branch will then be entitled to send members who live in the constituency, who pay the political levy and who are Labour Party members, as delegates to the General Management Committee, i.e. the executive of each local Labour Party branch. This is the jumping off point from which resolutions go upwards to the National Executive of the Labour Party and the Labour Party Conference. Unions affiliated to the Labour Party can send delegates directly to the conference and so can CLPs so you can have a double say in making Party policy. (See page 51.)

The job of the conference is to draw up policies. These are placed before the country in an election manifesto drawn up by the National Executive and the Parliamentary committee to be carried out by the Labour Party if it wins the next election, so if you use this structure you get a chance to influence the Labour Party, its councillors and the MP locally. And you get the chance to influence what happens in politics nationally through influencing your MP and sending delegates to higher policy-making bodies of the Party.

You might say 'That sounds fine but it doesn't work. The last Labour government did little for the workers and our MP has never supported trade union action locally.' There may be a lot of truth in this. One problem has been that most Labour Party MPs are not prepared to accept democratic accountability to the party that put them in Parliament. They say that they are not answerable to their GMC but to all their constituents. Of course they never call meetings of all their constituents nor are they willing to stand as MP for the 'Constituents' Party' when it comes to election time. The second problem is that Labour governments have often not seriously tried to carry out conference policy. In fact they argue that the government is not bound by conference decisions. However, recent conference decisions will introduce more democracy into the Labour Party and make it much easier for Constituency Labour Parties to replace their MPs or candidates. Many unions are not as democratic as they should be but they are an essential means of furthering our interests. Workers don't give up. They stay in and try to change them. The same is true of the Labour Party, which is the political arm of the trade unions. For any workplace organization it is an essential means of exercising influence in the interests of the members. Moreover, the last few years have shown that change is possible.

You should ensure that you take up your full quota of delegates on all relevant GMCs. You should do your best to see that the GMC acts in the interests of your members and that the MPs behaviour is monitored so that he does the same. If your union, for example, is opposed to an incomes policy and your MP votes for it, take it up with him before the GMC. If his record is consistently bad over a period of time you can try to gain enough support to set the removal process in motion. You will be surprised how many MPs change under pressure. Make sure that motions are regularly sent to the GMC from your branch and that delegates report back to the branch from the GMC. If there is an important strike or demonstration make sure the local Labour Party supports it with manpower and resources. Make sure the MP appears on picket lines and supports the union in the local press and on the radio. If you work in local government you will be able to exercise pressure on the councillors through the GMC. Many trade unionists lobby MPs or councillors when they face redundancies and cuts. Your MP or councillors will listen more closely if you talk to them from a position of strength within the Party.

To sum up, your workplace organization needs to use every possible lever of power it can to further and protect the interests of its members. What happens in the Labour Party locally and nationally affects those interests. You have the right to a voice and a piece of the action in terms of these decisions. *Take it!*

Agreements

The detailed agreements your stewards and committees win, backed by the membership, represent either the healthy glow or the deathlike pallor of a workplace organization. They can be good or bad depending on the strength of your organization and the skill of your negotiators. Agreements which lay down terms and conditions of work, pay, hours, sickness arrangements, holidays, time off for union duties and health and safety are called *substantive agreements*.

Agreements which describe the methods by which decisions are to be arrived at are called *procedure agreements*.

There are two points which you should always be considering at your workplace. Firstly, are you negotiating over every area that affects your life at work? You want a situation where almost nothing is decided unilaterally by management, where all decisions are taken through negotiation and embodied in agreement. Have you got an agreed scheme on maternity leave and pay? If so, what about paternity leave? If so, what about a workplace crèche? You bargain about money and hours but what about the wider matters that affect your job such as recruitment, or sales and investment. *Never* stop thinking about new areas that you want made the subject of agreement otherwise you are going backwards.

Secondly, where you have agreements, keep pushing the frontiers forward. Try to extend your rights by establishing custom and practice and interpretations of the agreement that are favourable to you. An agreement on time off for stewards can look very tight and restrictive on paper. Through years of extending it by custom and practice, stewards can spend as much time on union business as is necessary.

Don't get the idea that you should have a detailed *written* agreement on everything. Where you have carved out an area of independence, management will often want to write things down to try and restrict you. Always decide what works best in the union's interest.

Finally, don't think that agreements are sacred or give you any guaranteed protection. Many employers believe agreements are made to be broken. Agreements are, as Hugh Scanlon once said, temporary truces expressing the balance of power at a particular point in time – the rest period between rounds. Once one side feels strong enough it will return to the attack if it feels that the agreement was imposed by brute force.

Each workplace should have separate discipline and grievance procedures. We now look briefly at what this involves and then look at the kind of points your substantive and procedural agreements should cover in a few other important areas. The list is not exhaustive. For example, we have already seen that you might want agreements on time off for union activities and disclosure of information. (See pages 119 and 130.)

Discipline and dismissal

We have stressed that discipline and dismissal are conflict issues. Your view of what kind of conduct justifies disciplinary action will often be different from the employers'. Because of this, unions have tried to protect their members by limiting the employer's right to take such action. In the last ten years, the law has intervened in this area also.

In the past, unions were often opposed to disciplinary procedures on the grounds that they institutionalized management's 'right' to discipline workers and provided a method of 'proving' that they had done this in the proper way. However, given the legal changes, one of which is that employees should be given details of any disciplinary procedure thirteen weeks after starting work, and the publication of the ACAS code of practice on disciplinary procedures, most managements have produced some form of written procedure.

It is important that you distinguish between rules and procedures. Rules are statements such as: 'Proven theft will lead to instant dismissal.' Don't agree such rules with management. If you do so it may inhibit the union in challenging them later. Unions don't accept that all theft should lead to instant dismissal. There is a difference between a small theft

143

and a large one, between the man who has worked for the employer for a week and the man who has worked there thirty years. Let management draw up whatever rules it wants; the union should deal with each case on its merits. A procedure simply outlines the steps management have to follow when disciplining a worker. The union should insist that any disciplinary procedures are negotiated.

Right at the start, the union should make certain principles clear. Managements often say that 'instant dismissal' should be the penalty for gross industrial misconduct such as theft or fighting. Trade unionists believe that instant dismissal should never happen. Even if theft is admitted, there should be a full investigation. The worker should at least be given the chance to put his side of the story after consultation with the steward and be entitled to a hearing to argue any mitigating circumstances.

In this kind of case the code of practice suggests suspension for a short period. In a situation such as fighting, you may find this acceptable, but remember that once a worker is out of the workplace it can create an atmosphere of guilt, make it more difficult to put the case and gain support for it among workmates. What should be totally opposed is suspension without pay as a straight disciplinary weapon. For example, any Ford employee who fails to carry out an instruction of a supervisor is sent home and loses his wages for the shift and also the following shift, as well as his attendance allowance. This puts a lot of power in management's hands and is much more painful than a warning. Unions should also oppose any attempt to use fines or deductions from wages as a disciplinary weapon. The system by which workers who are late are fined, is much worse than the more usual system where they are simply warned. The Truck Acts limit the situations in which fines can be made.

Where you are negotiating a disciplinary procedure, you should press for the following points:

● A system of verbal and written warnings. The more warnings which have to be given before dismissal, the greater the protection the procedure affords to the employee.

144

- A right of appeal for disciplined employees. Often the most effective way is to appeal from the disciplinary procedure through the grievance procedure (see below).
- The right of the worker to be represented by a steward at every stage of the procedure. This means that the steward can argue the case against discipline right from the verbal warning stage. The agreement should clearly make it managements' duty to *ensure* that the steward is present before any interview takes place.
- Allow time to improve. You shouldn't be warned on Monday, then warned again on Tuesday and sacked on Wednesday. There should be a cooling off period to give the worker a chance.
- Time limits. Warnings should be wiped from the record after a reasonable period, say six to nine months.
- An employee's immediate supervisor shouldn't have the authority to dismiss. There should be a right of appeal to a level of management not previously involved in the case.
- Trade union representatives should not sit on a management disciplinary panel.

You may ask, can the law help in dismissal cases? In theory it can, but in practice it often doesn't. The law says that an employer must 1) have a satisfactory reason for sacking a worker, and 2) be able to show to an industrial tribunal that he acted reasonably in treating this reason as sufficient to warrant dismissal rather than a lesser penalty. To show that he has acted reasonably, the employer will have to have followed a reasonable disciplinary procedure along the guidelines laid down in the ACAS code of practice on disciplinary procedures. We would emphasize again that the law is very much a last line of defence in dismissal cases. Only a minority of sacked workers win their cases, and of those that do, *less than 1 per cent actually get their job back*; the rest just get some financial compensation.

A grievance procedure

A disciplinary procedure should protect you when management comes gunning for you. The more warnings you are entitled to, the better protected you will be. It's a different story when you have some complaint against management. Then it is you who wants action fast. You will need a procedure for processing your individual and collective grievances to management. Here, the fewer stages you have to go through the better. In the past, workplace grievances often had to go through stages outside the workplace if the procedure was part of a national agreement. But today, more and more grievance procedures are tailored to the individual workplace. You should note the following points:

● Ensure that your grievance procedure is negotiated with the union and has not simply been imposed by the management, and that it does not limit the kinds of problems that can be taken through the procedure.

● Management will want a commitment that no industrial action will be taken until the procedure is exhausted. You should aim to make any such commitment as vague as possible. There will be situations where even with a speedy procedure there will be problems which may require action, for example, where the heating is inadequate in wintertime.

● The procedure should provide that after the last stage at the workplace, the union may have the right to take the matter further, but after that one external stage the union will have the right to take industrial action.

● The procedure should ensure that each level of management which deals with a grievance should have the authority to settle that grievance. If you have to raise problems with a foreman who has no power to settle the matter, it is a waste of time to do any more than inform him. The procedure should provide access to the appropriate level of management who can resolve it. 'Paper stages' in a procedure delay problems being dealt with and demoralize the work-force. Work out who is the right manager to handle each stage.

● There should be time limits attached to each stage. In the example in Figure 5 the member first raises the problem with a supervisor. There are then two days for the supervisor to settle it before the worker can move to the next stage. Time limits like this stop management stalling.

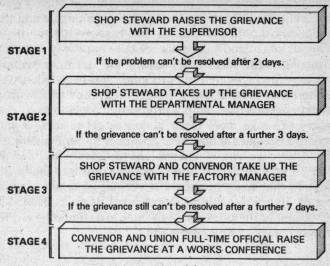

Figure 5. A typical grievance procedure

● Suppose management say that they are increasing the production targets of a section or moving a piece-worker to a less productive machine. Should the change be allowed to take place while the union is taking this problem through procedure? Not likely! Management would gain an advantage without proving their case. What you need to prevent such a situation is a 'status quo' clause in your procedure. This means that matters stay as they are until the management and union have agreed on the change or until the problem has been taken through the procedure. Here is an example of such a clause:

It is agreed that in the event of any difference arising which cannot immediately be disposed of then whatever practice or agreement existed prior to the difference shall continue to operate pending a settlement or until the agreed procedure has been exhausted.

Status quo clauses are an important limitation on managerial prerogatives. But they can't solve everything. One major

147

problem that often crops up is how the 'status quo' is interpreted. Unscrupulous managements may introduce changes without consultation and then when the union objects claim that the changed situation represents the status quo and that negotiations should proceed on that basis. What the union in a highly organized workplace seeks to impose is *mutuality*, i.e. management cannot implement any changes without union agreement, even if the procedure has been exhausted.

It should be argued that an effective, speedy procedure is in management's interest. If a procedure takes too long, then workers will take more direct action to get results. If your procedure becomes ineffective, reform it by renegotiating it or by short-circuiting it. Go straight to those who have the power to take decisions and settle grievances. Finally, it's important that workers should never negotiate about grievances or discipline without the steward being present. The requirement of the presence of the steward should be written into every stage of any agreement.

Health and safety agreements

In some workplaces the safety representative and the shop-steward will be the same person; in others different people will do the two jobs. Either way, safety representatives are union representatives and should be part of the process of collective bargaining at the workplace.

There will be a need to negotiate on substantive issues involving health and safety, for example, noise levels, atmospheric pollution or machine guarding. Such issues are discussed in detail in a companion book in this series, *Health and safety at work* by D. Eva and R. Oswald.

Safety representatives are given certain legal rights and functions under the Safety Representative and Safety Committee Regulations, 1978; for example, to inspect the workplace at least once every three months, to investigate members' complaints and to time off with pay to carry out such functions. It will be to the trade union's advantage if these rights can be extended through a negotiated safety agreement. Among the points this should cover are:

- Management agreeing to supply all relevant information on health and safety, including future plans, technical information on all hazards, accident and sickness figures, health and safety test results.
- Facilities, including not only those required by stewards (see page 128) but also library facilities containing Acts of Parliament, regulations, Health and Safety Executive publications, journals and reference books.
- Adequate time off with no loss of pay to carry out all necessary functions and to attend training courses.
- Adequate protective equipment and a procedure for its issue.
- The frequency of and procedure for carrying out routine inspections, for example, once per month, and the right to inspect immediately after any accident. Right of access to technical equipment is also essential.
- The right of the safety representative, wherever he feels there is a serious risk of injury, to stop the work until the problem can be investigated.
- The composition and items of reference of any joint union management safety committees.
- Procedures for dealing with safety grievances; e.g. if there is a dangerous problem act at once. Don't allow a status quo clause to be used by management to delay things. They may try to argue that unsafe or unhealthy conditions should persist until an agreement is negotiated – that is, until procedure is exhausted. You should completely reject any such manoeuvres.

Agreements on new technology and change in the workplace

'The new technology has been described as the 'second industrial revolution'! We have to ensure that unlike the first industrial revolution this second revolution now upon us will not trample underfoot the welfare and interests of those directly affected in the process of change.'

Len Murray, 1979.

Micro-electronics are already being introduced in a variety of ways across industry and commerce. Some of the more common applications include:

- word processors or 'computerized typewriters', allowing one operator to do the work previously done by three or four typists;
- data processing in which all the information now kept in filing cabinets and recorded on paper is stored electronically;
- computer aided design which is changing the work of draughtsmen and designers;
- automated machine tools which reproduce the operations of a skilled craftsman;
- robots which perform a variety of repetitive tasks such as welding, assembling or paint spraying.

Even if *your* workplace hasn't been affected yet, there is no room for complacency. By the time micro-electronics are applied it may be too late to negotiate about them. Moreover, the introduction of new technology is often preceded by new systems of working. Therefore you need to examine carefully management's motives for any changes in the organization of the workplace. The best way of guaranteeing that trade unions are fully involved in negotiating about technological change from the word go is to draw up an agreement on new technology as soon as it is even hinted at.

Obviously the detailed working out of agreements will vary with the particular circumstances in each workplace; but you should consider the following general points:

- Any changes to be on the basis of mutual agreement between management and unions, backed by a status quo clause. This will involve negotiations *before* any new equipment is purchased.
- Full information to be provided by management on a regular basis.
- No redundancies and no job loss through 'natural wastage'.
- Income levels to be maintained with increased payments if jobs involve new skills and responsibilities.

150

- Re-training to be given in new skills, at no loss of earnings.
- A reduction in the hours of the working week – to a four-day, thirty-hour week, and the elimination of systematic overtime.
- Negotiations to take place on the design of jobs to ensure job satisfaction and eliminate routine and boredom.
- No information derived from the new system to be used for measuring work performance.
- New health and safety hazards to be taken into account; for example, there may be a need to negotiate regular breaks to avoid stress or eyestrain.
- Review procedures should be built into the agreement; trial periods may be necessary.
- Disputes arising from the introduction or application of any new system should be processed through the existing grievance procedure.

We have to conclude, however, that the broad problems associated with new technology – unemployment, loss of job control, and deskilling – won't be solved through new technology agreements on their own, no matter how good they are. They may simply protect one group of workers at the expense of others. A full-time official, for example, who is responsible for two competing factories, only one of which can afford new technology, may negotiate a 'good' agreement there and so condemn his members at the other plant to unemployment. Trade unions by themselves can't solve this problem. The solution can only take place at a political level. As we've already argued, that's why involvement in the Labour Party is so important.

Redundancy agreements

Many trade unionists argue that a redundancy agreement on procedure and benefits implies that redundancy is acceptable. It focuses the members' minds on the issue as being inevitable someday and makes it more difficult to fight when it does arise. Others argue that it's best to negotiate a detailed agreement *before* redundancy occurs as your bargaining strength will be weaker when you are actually facing the situation. However, if your bargaining position is all that weak your employer may disregard the agreement anyway.

Redundancy agreements can be dangerous. They are best avoided. No worker should have the right to sell a job. The only real answer is an all out fight against redundancy. If this isn't possible and you do decide to negotiate such an agreement, then it should cover the following points.

The first stage should consist of a requirement on the management to satisfy the trade unions that there is in fact a manpower problem. Only once this justification from management is secured, should the unions agree to consider solutions. They should first deal with measures to *avoid* any redundancies. This could involve cutting working hours, halting recruitment, abolishing overtime, stopping sub-contracting, and implementing work sharing. The agreement should provide for management to inform the union *now* about future manpower and technology requirements, proposed investment and the development of new products and markets.

The Employment Protection Act provides for *minimum* periods of consultation by the employer with the union – at least 90 days if 100 or more are to be sacked over a period of up to 90 days, at least 30 days if between 10 and 100 are to be sacked over a period of up to 30 days; if less than 10 are to be sacked then at the earliest opportunity. You should try to improve on this and get the employer to agree that no individual dismissal notices will be issued until the consultation period is exhausted. Make sure all workers to be made redundant are allowed adequate time off to look for new jobs.

Ensure that the minimum periods of notice which the Employment Protection (Consolidation) Act guarantees workers – up to twelve weeks for twelve years of continuous service – are improved on. You should also consider the Temporary Employment Subsidy by which the government pays your employer to keep you in work.

All workers are not covered by the redundancy payments

provisions – you need a minimum of two years continuous service. The agreement should cover *all* employees.

The state redundancy payments are peanuts – you need to aim to treble and quadruple the legal minimum entitlements for each year of service. You should also try to improve some other problematical aspects of the legislation, for example, the fact that you lose your right to payment if you refuse 'suitable alternative employment'.

Some workers in industries such as steel and shipbuilding have negotiated a continuing payment for redundant workers while they remain unemployed, as well as an initial lump sum payment. One method would be for the employer to agree to top up the difference between unemployment benefit and past average earnings for six months.

If possible, agreements should provide for retraining with income maintained at past levels for the training period. This could also be negotiated for workers attending government retraining courses.

You should also consider including in the agreement provision for allowances such as travel and removal costs and rent for temporary accommodation when a new job is found.

Organizing the unemployed

The unemployed are the casualties of the fight against the attempts of the employers and the state to make workers pay for an economic crisis which is not their responsibility.

- If these workers are lost to the trade union movement, they will weaken the bargaining power of that movement.
- Unemployed workers have specific problems in terms of rights, benefits and entitlements. The union can help.
- Young workers who have never had a job may mature with no experience of the trade unions. Even worse, they may be influenced by fascist groups such as the National Front.

For these reasons, trade unions should ensure that workers remain members when they are unemployed. We should also attempt to recruit unemployed workers who perhaps have never been union members. The organized unemployed can increase the strength of the union movement. The weight of those still in work can be used to help the unemployed fight their own battles to secure welfare benefits as well as campaigning to secure measures which will reduce unemployment.

Check your union rules to see what the position is regarding members who are sacked. Most unions provide for existing members who are unemployed to remain in membership. In some unions unemployed members pay reduced subscriptions but receive all normal benefits. In others there is an option to pay full dues and receive full union benefits, or to pay a reduced fee and receive limited benefits and services. Sometimes there is a time limit, say a year, on unemployed membership. Some unions still provide specific benefits for unemployed members. Do you need to make rule changes in your union to cater for the unemployed? What practical steps are taken to prevent members dropping out when sacked?

There is a bigger problem presented by those who have not been union members when they were made redundant. Only a few specialized unions, such as the actors' Equity, provide for joining on the basis that somebody normally works in their recruitment area. In many unions you have to pay full dues for a period before you become entitled to services and benefits. Most unions will need to change their rules to cater for workers in this situation.

At the moment, there is a lot of discussion of these problems. It has recently been suggested that:

- centres for the unemployed should be set up in towns and cities where the unemployed can meet and discuss their specific problems;
- the unemployed should attend special TUC education courses to help with their problems;
- unemployed workers should be direct members of the TUC.

The first two suggestions are valuable but the third would

be extremely difficult to implement and would be no effective substitute for direct membership of individual unions. In Liverpool, for example, TGWU factory branches have kept going after closure. They have been switched to the general workers trade group and are, in effect, branches for the unemployed.

There are some very real problems, however. How are unemployed branches to be financed? How will they be serviced by full-time officers? Will there be a problem of unemployed members influencing decisions which only affect those still at work? Nevertheless, these problems must be overcome if the unemployed are not to be used to split and weaken the trade union movement while their own benefits are reduced still further, as happened in the 1930s. There are a number of points to be raised.

● What is your union's policy on the unemployed?
● Look carefully at your rule book. For example in the TGWU, while you normally need thirty-nine weeks at full rates to attain benefits, there is a special category for those under eighteen which could apply to the young unemployed. Your union executive may be able to give an authoritative interpretation of the rules if your rules revision conference is a long way off.
● Should there be special branches for the unemployed or is it better that they should attend what would be their relevant branch if at work?
● How can you recruit unemployed workers? What is the best approach? Leafletting the dole offices? Who should you recruit? Those who have registered for work in the categories in which your union organizes?
● What have you got to offer the unemployed? Can you help them to find jobs in your industry? Has the union got the knowledge to advise them on benefits or help with representation before appeals tribunals?
● Is there any possibility of establishing an unemployed centre in your area and providing education courses in it?
● What campaigns can unite and link the unemployed and the employed in the labour movement? For example, the

155

demands for a shorter working week, longer holidays and earlier retirement, which can both preserve existing jobs and create new ones.

As you can see from this chapter, shop-stewards have one hell of a job on their hands. You can see one reaction in the 'prayer' reproduced on page 157.

Further reading

If you want a very readable description of how to go about building a workplace organization do your best to get hold of H. Beynon, *Working for Ford* (E. P. Publishing, 1975). A useful recent pamphlet on combine committees is 'Trade Union Strategy In the Face of Corporate Power – the Case for Multi-Union Combine Shop-Stewards Committees' (Joint Forum of Combine Committees, 1980). For some advice on how trade unions can use the Labour Party, see A. Taylor and J. Fyrth, *Political Action* (Arrow, 1979). Health and Safety agreements and the Safety Representatives Regulations are examined in D. Eva and R. Oswald, *Health and Safety at Work* (Pan, 1981). The whole issue of control at work, and how trade unions can encroach on management decisions, is analysed in P. Burns and M. Doyle, *Democracy at Work* (Pan, 1981). There is little to help the unemployed trade unionist, but you could try J. Fulbrook *Social Security* (Sweet and Maxwell).

The Shop-Steward's Prayer
After An Old Folklore

Grant me O Lord, the genius to explain to my Brothers
the policies and plans of our great Union –
Even though no one explains them to me.
Give to me the intelligence, the wisdom and the
knowledge to understand the new techniques
applicable to our industry so that I may evaluate their
impact on my Brothers –
Even though no one shows me these techniques, no
one shows me how to evaluate them, and no one is
quite sure if they are, in fact, of any value at all.
Give to me understanding that I may –
Forgive the apathetic member,
Curb the over-ambitious member, and
Accept the views of the member who does nothing
until I have done something and then tells me how I
should have done it and what I should have done.
Make me formidable in debate, logical in argument,
fearless in confrontation; lawyer, actor,
mathematician, sage, philosopher, sociologist and
economist; pleading, cajoling, threatening,
belabouring, so that I may make –
The best of a good case and
A good case from no case at all.
Teach me, O Lord to stand with both feet firmly on
the ground
Even though I haven't a leg to stand on.
Oh Lord, let my Brothers see the future as a great
Brotherhood of men and, when they at last believe
in it,
Give me the physical strength to stop the punch-ups
that ensue –
Lord, I am a Shop-Steward; I pray you, in your
Infinite Wisdom see my need for all these things
and, in your Great Mercy, grant them to me.
And when I have them Lord – MOVE OVER.

Chapter **Seven**

Basic skills for union members

To take part effectively in any social activity you need to know the ground rules and practise the basic skills. This applies just as much to being a good trade union member as it does to any other activity, be it football, angling or stamp collecting. We've already emphasized the importance of members playing a full part in the workings of their trade union if unions are to be genuinely democratic. But to do this you need to know the ropes. Lack of knowledge of union skills and techniques makes it harder for you to make your voice heard. So in this chapter we'll try to:

● outline the main rules for taking part in union meetings;

- give practical tips on speaking and making reports at meetings;
- suggest ways in which union members can help deal with problems in their workplace.

Taking part in meetings

At the start of the branch meeting the chairman read out the business to be discussed. The first item was the management's recent pay offer. There was general agreement that it was inadequate. Somebody moved that they should ban all overtime until the offer was improved. Jim was a new member. He didn't think an overtime ban would have much impact, but he hadn't had much time to think about the issue. Eventually the ban was agreed to. It was only during the break for drinks that Jim found out that many of his workmates felt the same way as he did. They all wanted strike action to bring the maximum pressure to bear, but they hadn't felt confident enough to propose this at the time. When Jim tried to raise this under 'Any other business' at the end of the meeting the chairman ruled him out of order.

We can draw several lessons from this example – there was a need to circulate the agenda and motions to members in advance, the members needed to know how to frame and move motions and the rules by which branch meetings were conducted. Let's look at these points in more detail.

Why do we need rules for meetings at all? Why can't people just sit around a table and have a sensible discussion? It just doesn't work. If union meetings are to take decisions that may affect people's livelihoods and conditions then they need to be run carefully and fairly. There will inevitably be differences and conflicts. The rules are the ring which ensures a fair fight and a clear decision. For example, everyone might have their own ideas on what should be discussed so first you need an agreed order of business – an agenda. Then to go through this business in an orderly manner rather than a verbal free for all, you need to follow certain basic rules.

The degree of formality with which the agenda is drawn up and the rules adhered to will vary according to the kind of meeting. The different kinds of meeting you might come across in the trade union movement will range from the informal section or office meeting, shop-stewards' committees, mass meetings of all employees, branch meetings, regional and national committee meetings, union annual conferences and the TUC's annual Congress. Obviously a meeting of six people in an office can be run much less formally than the TUC with over a thousand delegates discussing dozens of motions. Nevertheless, the general principles of an agreed agenda and accepted rules for discussion should be common to all.

We'll look first at the agenda. A typical agenda for a branch meeting might be arranged in the following way:

Apologies for absence
Confirmation of the minutes of the previous meeting
Matters arising from the minutes
Correspondence
Enrolment of new members
Committee reports
Delegates reports
Motions
Any other business (AOB)

Some union rule books specify in detail the order in which business will be taken, but most will follow this general pattern. The content and order of the agenda should be drawn up by the chairman and the secretary before the meeting takes place. If you want to have an item discussed you will have to get in touch with the secretary before the meeting. In some branches, such requests may have to be in writing. It's important that the agenda and any motions which have been tabled are typed out and circulated in advance to the membership. This allows members to consider the issues, prepare their positions, and so produces informed debate. It also prevents meetings being manipulated by members smuggling through motions. If the agenda and motions aren't circulated in advance, then one group may pack a badly attended meeting with its supporters and pass any motions they want. Some items may crop up after the agenda has been circulated. If they are urgent, then they can be put before the meeting as emergency motions. But you will usually need a two-thirds majority vote to get an emergency motion on the agenda.

An item's place on the agenda may influence how much discussion it will receive. If time is pressing, an item low down the agenda may never be reached or else get little time to be properly discussed. Opponents of a particular motion may talk a lot on other items so that it is never reached. By the end of a meeting numbers may have dwindled. Supporters of a motion should try and get it placed on the agenda at the most favourable time for proper discussion.

Before a meeting can even begin, there will usually have to be a quorum, a minimum number of members present. If a quorum is required, the number should be specified in the standing orders. The idea of a quorum is that meetings should be representative. However, sometimes quorums are very low, for example, five members out of a branch with a total membership of five hundred people.

At the start of the meeting, the minutes of the previous meeting must be read out, unless they have been circulated in written form. We need minutes because they provide a permanent record of the decisions taken at previous meetings. If we didn't have them there would be constant arguments of the 'We didn't decide that! Yes we did!' type. For this reason, minutes need to be precise and accurate. The minutes may simply record actual decisions taken; for example:

It was resolved that the branch affiliate to the Manchester Area Safety Committee.

Sometimes minutes are fuller, giving a brief description of the main points of the discussion as well as motions voted on; for example:

'It was moved by V. Jones, seconded by D. Purvis, that the branch affiliate to the Manchester Area Safety Committee. Among other benefits, this would give the branch access to specialist books and journals on health and safety. The motion was carried by thirty-eight votes to three.

The style of the minutes will vary from branch to branch.

They shouldn't be a detailed blow by blow account but an accurate summary.

A member who was present at the previous meeting must move that the minutes are a correct record of what was discussed and decided at that meeting and someone else must support or 'second' this. If any member wishes to challenge the accuracy of the minutes then they must do so then. If the error is accepted by the meeting then there is no need to submit any amendment. If the error is disputed, then the challenger should move an amendment to correct the minutes, again supported by a seconder. The amendment will be discussed and a vote taken. If the minutes have to be altered, then the minute passing them should be changed to 'that the minutes as amended be accepted as a correct record'. Note that at this stage in the meeting, only questions on the accuracy of the minutes can be raised. After the minutes have been accepted by the meeting as a true record, they will be signed by the chairman to indicate this.

The chairman will then ask if there are any 'matters arising' from the minutes. Some of the matters discussed at the previous meeting will probably be coming up under another item on the agenda and the chairman should make it clear if this is the case. If they aren't, this part of the agenda gives members the chance to ask if there has been any progress in connection with the issue previously discussed. However, it *isn't* an opportunity for an 'action replay' of the previous meetings debates and the chairman should intervene if it threatens to become this.

Under correspondence, the secretary will announce the various letters received since the last meeting. Probably only the most important will be read out in full to save time. Others can be passed round the meeting to be read by any interested members. Not all correspondence requires discussion. Some is simply for information and may be 'noted' by the meeting.

In many branches, new membership applications are discussed, often only 'formally' and briefly. If the new members are present, this provides a good opportunity to welcome them.

There may be reports from branch sub-committees or from branch officers, such as the treasurer on funds and expenditure. There may also be reports from delegates to other bodies such as trades councils and Constituency Labour Parties.

Discussion of the items on the agenda will be conducted according to the rules laid down in the branch's standing orders (you should be able to get hold of a copy from your branch secretary). Although these will vary in detail, the general principles are as follows.

All discussion and speaking for and against motions must be addressed to the chairman, even though you may be replying to a point raised by another member. This 'speaking through the chair' is particularly important when discussion is heated and several people want to raise points. It allows the chairman to control discussion, because members can only speak with his permission. Otherwise, meetings would fragment into a collection of separate conversations between members. Chairmen have a difficult job to do. They have to allow full discussion as well as ensure that the meeting gets through its agenda in the time allocated. For this reason, it's a common rule that no member is allowed to speak more than once upon the same subject (unless they are the mover of a motion). In addition, if the agenda is very crowded, the chairman may place a time limit on each speaker.

Although chairmen are supposed to be neutral, they will have their own views on the business before the meeting. And they are in a strong position to influence the way things are conducted. A good chairman will ensure that the meeting runs smoothly, with full participation by every member. Bad ones can completely dominate the meeting, presenting those motions they support in a favourable light or not allowing sufficient time to discuss those they disapprove of. In extreme cases, members can challenge the chairman's ruling, but you normally need a two-thirds majority to succeed. If you feel your union meetings aren't being chaired in a neutral way, you will have to mobilize support among the other members in advance to ensure that items are fairly discussed.

The most important way in which discussion is structured

and action decided upon is by putting a motion to the meeting. Each motion must be moved and seconded by two members present at the meeting. If there is no seconder, then the motion 'falls' and no further discussion takes place on it. This ensures that the meeting's time is not wasted on issues which only one member supports. If you're going to put forward a motion, you should discuss it with your workmates to see if they support it. You will need to think carefully about any objections they raise and try to find the answers.

A motion's wording is important. It should be as simple, brief and clear as possible without any room for misinterpretation. It should make clear recommendations for action. Remember to make sure that any action demanded is within the powers of the body to which the resolution will be sent. For example, its no use demanding that the union's divisional council call a strike if the national executive is the only body which can authorize strike action. (See pages 81–8.) Have a look at the following two resolutions and consider which one is more effective.

Resolution 1

This branch totally and utterly condemns the vicious and anti-working class policies of this reactionary Tory government. In particular, it condemns the crude use of mass unemployment and the anti-trade union Employment Act to undermine the legitimate aspirations of working people to a decent standard of living and to destroy the trade union movement. It recognizes that these policies represent the actions of a government devoid of any programme which deals with the present crisis of capitalism except at the expense of the working class and calls for a campaign for full-blooded socialist policies.

Resolution 2

This branch views with the gravest concern the latest official figures which show that the town has an unemployment rate of 15.5 per cent. It calls upon the Trades Council to:

1 Call a demonstration against unemployment and the present government's economic policies.

2 Mount a campaign of support for such a demonstration in all trade union branches, local workplaces and Labour Party organizations.

3 Publish a leaflet to be distributed on this demonstration outlining the causes of unemployment locally and nationally and publicizing the alternative economic strategy of the TUC.

The mover of a motion has the right to speak first. The mover should state the reasons for supporting the motion and answer any anticipated objections. This may pull the rug out from under any opponents. The seconder has a right to speak to the motion when seconding it, but can do this formally, without speaking. By doing this, the seconder retains the right to speak during the discussion. This can be a very useful tactic. The seconder can wait until the opposition builds up its arguments then swoop in to counterattack.

After the motion has been moved and seconded, the chairman will ask for speakers for and against the motion in turn to achieve a balanced debate. If there are none against, this suggests that the meeting is in general agreement and can move to the vote. After the discussion, the mover has the right to reply to the debate. This last word is a vital weapon. It should be used to summarize the arguments in favour of the motion and to counterpunch against the criticisms of the opposition.

Only one motion can be debated by a meeting at one time. However, some members may wish to change some of the words of the original motion or add or delete words. They can do this by moving or seconding an *amendment* to the motion. The mover of an amendment doesn't have the right of reply to discussion on the amendment, only to speak when introducing it. An amendment must be relevant to the original motion and shouldn't completely distort it. If the amendment negates the motion then the chairman shouldn't accept it. For example, take the motion 'that the branch supports the TUC's call for a Day of Action on 14 May and instructs all members to withdraw their labour on that day'. If a member moved as an amendment to 'delete all after 14 May' this would, in effect, rob the motion of its central point and cancel it out, so the chairman shouldn't accept it. If someone wanted to strengthen the motion by adding the words 'it also encourages all members to participate in the demonstration organized by the trades council on that day' they could move this as an addendum. If neither the mover nor anyone else present objected to this, it could be incorporated with the motion. If anyone objected it would have to be voted on as an amendment. Only one amendment to a motion can be discussed at any one time and this must be voted on before any other amendments are moved. The chairman should ask for notice of any amendments to the motion and then, if possible, take them one by one in the order that they affect the original motion.

Before votes are taken, the chairman should read out what is being voted on so that everyone has a clear idea of what is happening. The order in which votes are taken is important. If an amendment is voted down, then discussion can continue on the original motion. If the amendment is carried, then the original motion is altered accordingly and is referred to as the *substantive motion*. Further discussion can take place as necessary before going on to take the votes for and against the substantive motion. If the motion is passed, it then becomes a resolution of the meeting, i.e. a decision, and this will be recorded in the minutes. If any of the votes are evenly tied, the chairman may exercise a casting vote to decide the outcome, although he doesn't have to do so. Once an issue has been voted on, the standing orders will often specify a period of time before it can be brought before the branch again for further discussion. This rule is to prevent endless debate on any one subject and to stop branches reversing decisions month after month.

During discussions, members may raise points of order with the chairman. These can only relate to the conduct or the procedure of the meeting – for example, if there is a departure from the subject or a breach of standing orders. Points of order should be very brief. The chairman will then say whether it is upheld or not. Remember that you can't raise a point of order just because you disagree with what's being said.

During the discussion, a member who feels that the debate

166

has gone on long enough and who hasn't previously spoken may move a *procedural motion* 'that the question be put'. This takes priority over the original motion and if it is seconded it is immediately voted on. If the procedural motion is lost, the discussion continues as before. If it is carried, discussion on the original motion is ended and the chairman will ask the mover to sum up before going on to the vote. A more drastic type of procedural motion is to move 'next business'. If this is lost, discussion continues on the original motion. But if it is carried, the original motion and any amendments are thrown out without any vote being taken on them and the meeting moves on to the next item on the agenda.

All these points may seem complicated and unnecessary. At many meetings the business will be non-contentious and motions will be discussed without the need for points of order and procedural motions. But at times they are necessary to ensure the smooth running of a meeting. Although they may look intimidating at first, once you've mastered these general principles, you should be able to take part in any union meetings. For a fuller discussion of the points covered in this section see *Mr Chairman*, by Wal Hannington, Lawrence & Wishart, London, 1966.

Taking notes and making reports

Lucy was a home help and a member of NUPE. At her last branch meeting she had agreed to act as a delegate to a local action committee organizing a demonstration in support of abortion. She had attended the committee meeting three weeks previously and once more was attending her branch. But when it came to 'Delegates Reports' on the agenda, Lucy's mind went blank. She stumbled through her report, unable to recall exactly what had been decided at the committee and with only a hazy memory of the points discussed.

What went wrong? Why didn't Lucy say more? She made two mistakes. First, she didn't make any notes about what had taken place at the meeting. Secondly, she hadn't prepared what she was going to say in her report to the branch.

167

Taking notes and making reports are two important and related skills for union members to develop. We'll deal with each one in turn.

Notes

Taking notes is important in a number of situations:

● at meetings, so you can remember what was said;
● when you have to prepare a verbal report;
● when union representatives have to note down the facts of a grievance they have to handle;
● when union representatives have to prepare their case to present to management during negotiations.

Notes about meetings are useful for several reasons. They provide a permanent record of what went on. People's memories fade very quickly, especially where a lot of detail is concerned. The action of taking notes also forces you to concentrate on what is being said and will help you remember it later.

You have to be careful about the *amount* of notes that you take. There is no hard and fast rule about this. It will vary according to the content of what is being said and how familiar you are with the subject. For example, a report on a new pay agreement may require a lot of detailed notes; a talk on a union policy which you are well acquainted with might be much less detailed.

It is a mistake to try and take down every word that is said. Most people speak at a rate of about 130 words per minute, so unless you are a trained shorthand writer you won't be able to do this anyway. If you try, you will end up scribbling frantically and unable to concentrate on what's actually being said. Instead, you should aim to pick out the important points of fact and argument a speaker is making. It is often useful to do this by using headings and sub-headings, leaving plenty of space so that you can go back over your notes and make additional comments while the talk is still fresh in your mind. You should be listing the main topics and arguments, not just noting down interesting phrases.

With practice, you can soon develop your own 'shorthand' style of writing, using initials, abbreviations and symbols.

We can demonstrate some of these points by looking at the notes made during a talk by a union official on the subject of 'New Technology and Change in the Office' (see below and page 170). The *second* set provides a much clearer and effective record than the first. Compare them for yourself and see why this is the case.

> Notes of talk at Branch Meeting:
> New technology and automation will have big impact on office work — many jobs lost but some created. Need for the union to push for shorter working week to create more jobs — also to negotiate new technology agreements with company.

You can see that the second set of notes amounts to a skeleton outline – the 'bare bones' – of what the speaker said. From them, it is possible to follow the main topics discussed, the key points of the argument and some of the more important facts. You could look them over again in a few years time and still have a clear recollection of the main points of what was said at a branch meeting years earlier.

So far we've been talking about making notes at meetings. The same general principles also apply to taking notes from books and documents. Taking notes will help you to concen-

Branch Meeting 22/3/1981.
"New Technology and Change in the Office"
Speaker: Mrs A. Smith, Area Organiser,
        Union of Office Workers.

<u>Impact of New Tech.</u> Rapid increase, chip much
cheaper. <u>All</u> office work will be affected.
Especially hit <u>women</u>, young people, older
workers. 600,000 fewer clerical and
secretarial jobs by 1983. — New Tech. only
create about 10,000 jobs per year in U.K.
Applications include:
- word processors, esp. where lot of standard
  typing.
- direct entry of information via keyboards
  and optical character recognition.
- electronic internal mail.

<u>Union action</u>
- move to 30 hrs, 4 day week,
  larger holidays
- set up joint technology committees
  with other unions — site/company
  levels.
- Technology agreements to cover:
  - joint control
  - monitoring
  - no job loss
  - job content/satisfaction
  - job evaluation
  - training
  - health and safety

trate on the main points of what it is you're reading and provide a summary for future reference without having to read the whole book over again. Some tips which prove helpful are:

● Read through a chapter or document quickly to get the gist of what it says. Don't worry if you don't understand every word of it.
● Read it over again slowly to get a fuller understanding. You can underline the main points or phrases in each paragraph or section if the book or document belongs to you, otherwise jot them down in a notebook. Make a note of words or phrases that you don't understand, then look them up in a dictionary or ask a colleague what they mean.
● Try and write out a summary in note form of each chapter or section. But beware of going into too much detail; you will rarely need to copy out whole sentences, for example. Put down just enough to distinguish the important points.

Reports

Reports, both written and verbal, are a vital ingredient of trade union activity. Think of the range of occasions when reports are necessary. For example:

● from union officials to mass meetings;
● from branch delegates to trades councils, Constituency Labour Parties, divisional councils or annual conference;
● from branch officers to the branch members;
● from branch officers and shop-stewards to district committees and full-time officials;
● from workplace representatives to their own members.

You can probably think of other instances. But what is readily apparent is that such reporting is one of the most important channels whereby information flows down to the rank and file member or up to the full-time officials. Reports therefore play an important part in the working of unions as democratic and representative bodies. As we noted in an earlier

171

chapter, a crucial dimension of trade union democracy is the accountability of union officials to the members they represent – be they the shop-steward or the general secretary. In this process of accountability, members will only be able to exercise informed control on the basis of full reports of their officials activities. This is one reason why unions often publish the reports of full-time officials in their journals or circulate them to branches. Equally, full-time officials will only be able to reflect the wishes of their members if they are kept fully informed of workplace events through shop-stewards and branch officers reporting to them.

How do you go about making a report or preparing a speech to a union meeting? A little thought and preparation beforehand will pay great dividends. Some simple guidelines to follow are:

● Work out and write down roughly the main points that you want to make.
● Arrange these points into the order in which you want to make them.
● Rewrite your report in note form around these main headings.
● Follow a simple and logical structure of headings. Every report should consist of the general framework of:

Introduction – who you are if your audience doesn't already know;
– what you are going to talk about;
– why the subject is important.
Main headings – list the key points of information or argument.
Conclusion – summarize what you've said and suggest any relevant future action.

In short, you should 'tell them what you're going to say, say it, then summarize what you've said'.

● Don't make your notes too detailed. It usually isn't helpful to write out your speech in full. You'll end up just reading it out and this will be dull and uninteresting for your listeners. Your notes should be an *outline* of what you're going to say, not a complete script.

- Consider who it is you're speaking to. For example, if you are speaking about a workplace problem to your work-mates, you won't need to go into as much background detail as you would with people unfamiliar with your work situation.
- Ask yourself how much your audience knows about the subject already.
- Think carefully about the points that it is important for them to know.

Dealing with union members' problems in the workplace

Del, the shop-steward, returned to the office from lunch one Thursday afternoon. He found Connie, one of his members, in tears. She explained that two weeks before she had asked Mr Everly, the manager, to let her have the following Friday afternoon off to go on holiday for the weekend. 'He said he'd think about it,' she continued, 'and let me know, because we're a bit short staffed at the moment. Brenda was there, she'll tell you. I didn't hear any more about it so I went to remind him that I wouldn't be in tomorrow afternoon. He said that he'd never given me permission. But the tickets are booked so I told him I'd go anyway and he said I'd be sacked if I did.' Del had only been the steward for a month and wasn't quite sure what to do, but felt he had to do something. 'Right,' he said, 'we'll soon sort out Mr Everly.'

'This business with Connie,' he began in the manager's office, 'she's assumed you had no objection to her going because you didn't get in touch and now she's spent money on tickets.'

'Hang on,' said the manager, 'what I said was that she was fifteen hours in deficit on her flexitime and she's used up all her annual leave. And the department is short staffed because two people have been off. I told her that if they came back then I might view her request favourably, but just then I couldn't consider it. When she came in again today I told her that it still wasn't on. She announced that she'd take the time off anyway. She was warned once before about taking time off so I told her that she'd be going too far.'

The manager called Connie into the office and began going over his version of events. 'We've gone through all this before,' interrupted Connie. 'Let's hear him out,' said Del. 'Whose side are you on,' retorted Connie, 'I'm taking tomorrow afternoon off and that's that.' So saying she stormed out. 'If she takes time off she's sacked,' said the manager. 'Oh well, I suppose you're right, Mr Everly,' muttered the embarrassed steward.

So Del didn't sort it out. His lack of experience and forethought led him to make a series of mistakes which ended up in a worse situation than before. Obviously this example is a bit exaggerated. Its unlikely that one individual would do so badly. But by analysing what went wrong in this case we can outline the general principles of how members and their stewards can handle problems at work and how they should go about dealing with management.

Get the facts of the case

Del got off to a bad start because he wasn't in possession of all the facts. Members can help their representatives by giving them as much information as they can about their particular problem – the names of people involved or who might have seen something, the actual events of the case, where and when it happened, who said what. Even if some piece of information may not mean much to the member, it might appear significant to the steward who will have a broader view of what's going on in the workplace. Members may not offer all these facts automatically and the steward will often have to question them carefully to get all the relevant points out of them. This stage of interviewing the member is crucial. If a steward fails to get the facts clear at this stage, it can cause serious misunderstandings, as Del found to his cost.

Although the steward often needs to ask probing questions, its very important that the member is put at ease and that a relaxed and confidential atmosphere is established. Members will often be upset about a particular problem. The steward will have to calm them down before beginning the interview. Where the interview takes place is important in this respect. A member won't feel like discussing personal matters in the middle of a crowded office. For this reason, access to a room where members can be interviewed is an important facility for stewards (see page 128).

The steward shouldn't appear hostile or suspicious even if the member's story appears to be incredible. Sometimes apparent discrepancies will crop up in the member's version of events. The steward will need to probe these sensitively. But remember, it's neither an interrogation nor a cross-examination. If the steward antagonizes members then they may well be less forthcoming. At the end of the interview, the steward should go over the story again to make sure that the facts are clear. The steward shouldn't make any promises to the member. Never say 'it's in the bag' until it is. Always make arrangements with the member as to what's to be done next.

Check the facts with others

Memories are never 100 per cent reliable. Sometimes, perhaps to put ourselves in a better light, we may distort the facts we report. To make absolutely sure of the facts, the steward should check them wherever possible with witnesses. If Del had had a quiet word with Brenda he would probably have got a fuller version of the story and he would have been in a much better position to assess the situation.

Decide what action is necessary

Once the steward is in full possession of accurate information then a decision will need to be made about what action to take if any. The facts will have to be measured against the precedents of custom and practice in the workplace, against any relevant legal standards and analysed within the context of trade union organization. In a case of dismissal, for example, a steward should compare the facts of the case against previous dismissals, examine whether the disciplinary procedure had been strictly adhered to, consider whether the code of practice on disciplinary procedures and the law on unfair dismissal had been breached, weigh up the amount of support for the threatened member and how strong a bargaining position the union was in at that particular time. In Connies' case, Del should have found out if there had been allowances of time off in similar cases in the past, he should have ascertained the degree of sympathy for Connie in the office and how far the members were willing to support her, and he should have considered the disciplinary implications of management threatening members with the sack in this way. Once he had decided to raise the matter with the manager, he should have clearly explained to Connie what he was going to do, what he thought the chances of success were and what compromises might need to be made so that her hopes weren't raised too high, and he should have arranged to meet her after his meeting to report back on the situation.

A steward will also have to consider the possible repercussions of an individual's case on the interest of other members and other sections of the work-force. This may mean consulting with fellow stewards, the convenor or the branch secretary. For example, had there been numerous other instances of abuse of the flexitime system in Del's office and management were threatening to review its operation, Del might have decided not to take Connie's case up for fear of the wider ramifications.

If the steward does have to knock back a member on taking up a grievance, it's important that an explanation is given as to *why* it shouldn't be taken up. If the member isn't satisfied then the steward can offer approaching the convenor or a union official for their opinion. Such an offer will usually convince most members that the steward isn't talking with a forked tongue. Stewards shouldn't allow themselves to be always taking up hopeless cases. They have a duty to represent their members, but not under *any* circumstances. If a steward loses credibility with management as a result of such grievances then it's not in the members' collective interest, whatever disgruntled individuals might think.

Prepare the case

It's vitally important that stewards and members prepare the case before going in to meet management. This will involve marshalling all the key points, working out which are the strongest arguments in favour of the member and deciding on what your aims are, i.e. what you want to get out of the meeting. In all but the simplest cases this is best done by preparing written notes. In setting the aims, the steward and the member may well agree that they won't get everything that they ask for so they will work out a fallback or compromise. Some argue that this can build defeatism into the negotiations and that it's better just to stick to your initial target throughout. Either way, it's important to have a clear idea about what sort of outcomes are acceptable before meeting the management side. It's difficult to do this thinking on your feet during the actual meeting. You need to anticipate what management will be thinking, what their response will be to the union's case, how you can reply to their counter-arguments, what compromises will be acceptable to them and how much authority they have within the enterprise to make an agreement.

In our case study, Del would have tried to get Connie the time off, although she hadn't made this easy for him. He could plan to point out the confusion created by the manager leaving the situation open ended, Connie's generally good work record and the importance of maintaining good working relationships with the staff. He might expect the manager to raise the problem of the other workers being off and could try to counter this by pointing out that staffing levels must be too low if the office couldn't cope with such day to day problems; the threat of the union pressing for a review of staffing levels might also have put pressure on the manager. But given the weakness of her position Connie might have to be prepared to give an undertaking to reduce her flexitime deficit within a specified period or agree to work late that day to clear some of her workload.

Meeting management

When meeting management you should adopt a polite but firm manner. It's important that new stewards shouldn't let managers patronize, or browbeat or soft-soap them. If an unequal negotiating relationship is established it may be difficult to change. It's always essential for a steward to take along another member or fellow steward when meeting management on union business. This provides a witness to the negotiations. It protects the steward from any possible charge of doing deals behind the members' backs and prevents an unscrupulous manager from going back on any agreement reached. In addition, two heads are usually better than one. If a steward is handling an individual member's grievance, it is a matter of judgement and tactics whether or not that member should accompany the steward. If the member involved *does* meet management, then they should be carefully briefed beforehand by the steward.

In our example, Connie didn't understand what Del was trying to achieve and her outburst greatly weakened her position. If anything unexpected does happen in such a meeting, then the union side should ask for an adjournment. No one can prepare for every eventuality and they may need to review their objectives and tactics. If this isn't done, then the union side may blunder on, giving contradictory or conflicting responses which management can exploit. In any negotiations a united front is essential, with the steward acting as spokesperson, unless the steward calls on the member to speak.

During the course of the meeting the union side should keep its target objective firmly in mind and avoid being sidetracked (notes can often act as a focus here). If an offer is made, the steward should ask for an adjournment at once to discuss the matter. If an agreement is reached, its terms should be clearly understood by both sides. If it's put in writing there will be less scope for future confusion. After the meeting the steward should discuss the outcome with the member and consider if any further action is necessary.

If these basic rules are followed by members and their

stewards, then workplace problems and grievances should be resolved more successfully. Obviously many negotiations are more complicated than the simple case we've described here. They may involve teams of stewards working together. But the general principles of collecting information and preparing the case will still apply. Not all negotiations will end in mutual agreement, however. If they break down, then the union side will have to consider what sanctions against the employer are necessary. In the next chapter we'll discuss the different types of industrial action and how they can most effectively be applied.

Chapter **Eight**

Industrial action

In a capitalist society the employers own the factories, offices, machinery and tools. Workers have to sell their labour to the employers in order to make a living. Even when the workers combine together in unions to bargain with the employer, he is still in a much stronger position. He can make workers redundant, close down his workplace and invest his capital elsewhere. The basic weapon that workers have to stop the employer behaving like a dictator is their ability to withdraw their labour and go on strike. We have already pointed out that many people see strikes as a social problem caused by breakdowns of communication or malevolent agitators who need controlling by law. This is rubbish.

Strikes are natural and inevitable. They simply represent the fact that the workers involved are saying to their employer we are withdrawing from our bargain with you, we are not prepared to work any longer for the wages and conditions that you are offering.

Strikes are an essential protection for workers. If you did not have the right to go on strike the employers would have a field day. Your talk would be cheap without any muscle to back it up.

The ability to take strike action is basic to effective trade unionism. In this chapter we look briefly at:

● the different kinds of industrial action and when to use them;
● how to organize your industrial action to make it as effective as possible;
● how the law is likely to affect you when you are engaged in industrial action.

Different kinds of industrial action

Going on strike, totally withdrawing your labour, is only the most obvious form of industrial action. You may hear the names of different kinds of strike bandied about. An official strike is a stoppage which is authorized by the union according to the rule book. An unofficial strike is a stoppage which, although it may in fact have union support, the workers have not yet been able to get formal support. Sometimes, however, it may be opposed by the union leadership. An unconstitutional strike is a situation where workers have taken action without first exhausting the agreed procedures with the employer if the procedure requires this. (See page 145.)

The bosses and the media from Scunthorpe to Sorrento are virulent in their condemnation of unofficial and unconstitutional strikes. However, grievance procedures are often so long and tortuous that workers are driven to strike to get a solution to a pressing problem. Moreover, a strike may lack official support because of the time taken to go through lengthy rule book procedures or because the relevant union bodies, far away from the situation, fail to see as the workers involved do, that action is essential. When we talk about strikes, however, we are talking about a wide range of action from the large scale, carefully planned confrontation between say miners or steel workers and the government to the lightning one hour stoppage as either part of a guerilla campaign or as a spontaneous one-off walk out because workers have simply had enough.

Sometimes workers may decide that they can cause problems for the employer without the loss of wages involved in a strike. They may decide to work to rule. This means going back to doing exactly what you are supposed to do in your job and cutting out the little extras that can make things go efficiently. They may decide to 'go slow' or work without enthusiasm, take constant toilet breaks, or, as in printing, call mandatory chapel meetings in working time. Other sanctions may be banning overtime or refusing to train newcomers.

How successful this kind of cut price action can be depends on the nature of your job and the state of the business at the particular time. If there is no overtime being worked or business is slack you may have little effect. However, the essential problem is that if you are successful then your employer will escalate the action. He is not going to be taken to the cleaners whilst you sit there grinning like a Cheshire cat. He will suspend individual after individual and hence in most cases drive you into full strike action.

● These types of industrial action need careful planning so that everyone involved knows exactly what they should or should not be doing and do not, for example, act too provocatively.
● They should generally be seen as preliminaries to full action and you should be prepared for escalation at any time. A good example of the use of the work to rule was by the miners in 1974. The Coal Board had fairly full stocks

182

of coal which would mean that a strike would take a long time to bite, at great cost to the workers. They therefore started a well-timed work to rule which ran down stocks and made the strike, when called, more effective. However, you should always be clear as to when this kind of action has outlived its utility. Workers may get so used to it they may not want to strike in the end! On the other hand, they may become demoralized and feel that the action is having little impact on the employer. The same problem can occur in a series of one-day strikes: people feel that they are losing money without getting anywhere.

Finally, three tactics you will need to think about in running industrial action, are the occupation or sit in, picketing and blacking.

Preparing industrial action

It is difficult to generalize here when we are dealing with the spontaneous explosion in which workers walk out, at one end of the scale, and the carefully planned set piece battle on the other. The first point, however, is to ensure that industrial action is necessary. Have you exhausted all other means of achieving your aims? Second, there are good and bad times for industrial action. You are obviously better placed when your employer has more business than he can deal with than in the situation when his order book is empty. However, if you are involved in an annual wage review and are faced with a derisory offer, you may have little choice. Third, in the relatively controlled situation make sure that all workers involved know what the dispute is about, what the union's demands are and what the attitude and stance of management is. This should be done by thoroughly discussing the matter before the workers' representatives approach management and by reporting back thoroughly on management's position.

Fourth, when you reach the brink and a strike looms, make sure that workers take an informed decision. This brings us to the vexed question of ballots. There is a whole range of different democratic methods used in the trade unions to see what members want. Some people argue that secret postal ballots should be used. However, in many situations it may be much better to vote on industrial action by a show of hands after there has been a full discussion of the issue involved. Direct voting makes it clear that democracy has responsibilities and requires some involvement. The problem with a postal ballot is that it stresses inactivity. You do not vote after a full debate, involving all those who are likely to be affected and who are responsible enough to attend the meeting. This may also provide *some* antidote to the blatantly distorted intervention of the Press in union decision making. Once the decision is taken, every worker's mind should be cleared of all doubts, whatever the rights and wrongs, whichever way you voted. Your job now is to take the action as effectively and as painlessly as possible. Joe Louis knocked out his great friend John Henry Lewis in the first round to spare him pain. Do the same to your employer and production will quickly be back to normal.

Fifth, if a stoppage occurs because of management provocation or because of a sudden 'explosion', make sure that individuals or small groups do not take action off their own bat. Try and make sure that if a particular incident blows up that there is a quick meeting of those involved or better still that the union 'trusties' in each section go immediately to other areas of the workplace to inform others workers what has happened so that a meeting of all workers can be arranged. You often need to buy a little time to think through the implications of the situation and there should be a thorough discussion so that the views and feelings of all workers can be made known and the correct approach can be thrashed out. It is important for the leaders to point out the basic issues and state the alternative courses of action. They should also attempt to guard against euphoria and false optimism and point out that often a long and bitter struggle will be ahead. A vote should then be taken. 'Unity is strength' is important here. If one group walks out then they may be isolated and outside the gates, whilst management can orchestrate a campaign to win the support of the remaining workers from inside.

Sixth, it is important to get the organization of the strike on the road as quickly as possible. Once a decision to go on strike has been taken you should immediately elect a strike committee small enough to be efficient, but large enough to represent all sections of workers involved. The strike committee should get the names, addresses and telephone numbers of all involved so that they can quickly get in touch with strikers. They should arrange a meeting of the strike committee as soon as possible to begin the day to day organization of the strike and arrange for a mass meeting of strikers immediately after this meeting so that the committee can report back and begin to delegate jobs to the strikers.

However, the strike committee should immediately organize a picket rota and ensure that pickets are placed on all gates and entrances straightaway. The more those working settle into a routine, the harder it becomes to shake them out of it. You must also keep going the momentum your initial action has achieved.

Problems with industrial action

Watching the television or reading the papers in the last few years, you might get the impression that picketing and blacking are hangovers from the Dark Ages and that workers involved in these activities are on the same level as Al Capone, Lucky Luciano or the Krays. There has also been a constant clamour for the law to be tightened to deal with these activities. Let us look at the matter a little more closely. When workers are able to completely close down a workplace, picketing and blacking are not important. They become important when, despite a stoppage, an employer is still able to keep production going. In this situation, every worker who goes into work is not just going into work, he is not just insisting on the right to earn a living. Whether he likes it or not, his action in going into work must help one side in the dispute, i.e. his employer. His action in going into work

185

must weaken one side, i.e. his fellow workers. So when trade unionists talk about the right to picket, they are talking about the right to persuade other workers that they are backing the wrong side and actively harming their fellows.

In the same way, a supplier of your employer who continues to deliver supplies is supporting your employer and undermining your bargaining power. The more production your employer can maintain, the weaker the position of the strikers. Just as a supplier may stand by your company because both of them are employers, so you should be entitled to ask the suppliers employees to refuse to handle work for your company and stand by you because you are all workers. They may also need your help some day. This is the justification for blacking. When workers occupy the premises they are again often attacked for interfering with the employer's property. But it can be argued that workers who spend a great part of their lives on these premises producing value for the employer have some justification for using these premises as a base when they are on strike.

It is unfortunate that, as we shall see later, workers have few *legal* rights to picket or black effectively, to the extent that the law makes life difficult here for workers it strengthens the employer. However, in practice workers are able to utilize these rights if they are aware and well organized; so let us now look at some of the tactics you will need to use where you are forced into taking industrial action.

The occupation In many strikes where you have strong support it is worth considering an occupation. This will not preclude the need for other methods such as blacking and picketing. It will provide a secure base for developing these tactics. A work-in is where, whilst occupying, the workers keep on working. A sit-in is a normal withdrawal of labour but you take over your workplace as strike headquarters. The sit-in has been by far the most common. The advantages are clear:

● you can directly stop blacklegging and movement of materials;

- you get more publicity;
- you are more comfortable than if you are picketing outside;
- you have more resources for conducting the dispute, holding meetings and maintaining morale;
- you are representing a direct challenge to your employer.

In most recognition disputes the stoppage is only partial and workers lack the confidence to occupy. It is, however, a tactic well worth considering. If you decide to occupy do so immediately. This gives management little room for manoeuvre and avoids splits in the work-force.

Blacking In most disputes over recognition the employer will be able to carry on production to some degree. Unlike a well-organized factory with a union tradition, those on strike may have limited knowledge as to customer suppliers. If this is the case then you will be more reliant on the outside union organization.

What you will be aiming at here is for workers who work at companies that supply your employer to refuse to handle any goods that are destined for your workplace, and for workers who work for your employers' customers to refuse to handle any goods that are brought into their workplace from your employer. Even if you have managed to stop production at your factory, companies which use your employer's goods may be able to get substitutes. To increase the impact of your stoppage you may wish to get these substitutes blacked so that your employer's customer will pressurize him to settle so that he can start getting deliveries.

There are two basic problems involved in blacking today. The first is that the judges have increasingly issued injunctions – legal orders – against unions, telling them that they must call off blacking as it is illegal. For example, the printing unions had a dispute over recognition with an anti-union employer, T. Bailey Foreman. Because they could not bring this employer to heel directly, they went to companies which advertised in T. Bailey Foreman's newspaper, the *Nottingham Evening Post* and asked them to stop their adverts. When some of them refused, the unions told their members on other newspapers not to handle adverts from these particular advertisers. The idea was to bring pressure on the advertisers in order to bring pressure to bear on the employer directly involved – TBF.

However, a number of the advertisers went to court and got an injunction, telling the union to call off their blacking as it was too far removed, the court said, from the initial dispute.

Secondly, properly organized blacking at times is a major operation. As Tony Beck says in his book on The Fine Tubes Strike,

The strike committee soon found that they totally lacked the enormous resources required to maintain the kind of checks needed to counter management's operations. The only thing that could have conceivably done so was the official union machinery.

Obviously, there can be problems in convincing workers who have no direct interest in a dispute to come into conflict with their own employer. In the Fine Tubes dispute, for example, Fine Tubes was the only company capable of producing a particular component for Rolls Royce. Blacking by Rolls Royce workers all over the country would probably have caused several hundred lay-offs. There was also a political situation as Rolls Royce was requesting money from a Conservative government to save jobs. Little seems to have been done by the AUEW and TGWU to push for blacking. As the Fine Tubes strike committee said in their final statement,

In several crucial cases we came across shop-stewards and convenors who for reasons best known to themselves did not black Fine Tubes: in particular, Rolls Royce, Derby; Osborn Steels Group, Bradford; Henry Wiggins, Hereford; UKAE; BAC of Preston; all 100 per cent organized firms who thus left crucial loopholes . . .

This illustrates how far flung can be the workers who those on strike for recognition will be asking for support. Obviously, there are vast problems if everything is left to the strikers themselves and they have to travel hundreds of miles to make contacts with other shop-stewards. The matter can initially be dealt with more efficiently if the full-time officials responsible for the strike get in touch with their opposite numbers who look after the workplace whose cooperation you are seeking.

Experience shows that workers, if given a lead and a convincing case, are often able to look beyond their own sectional interests and black goods in order to help fellow trade unionists. However, it seems as if, at times, union officials take too pessimistic a view of the situation and do not take a sufficiently vigorous line in prosecuting blacking. In the Grunwick dispute, for example, whilst the postmen were prepared to black Grunwick, their leaders took action to stop them doing this. You should push your full-time official all the way. If you are not getting anywhere then you may have to escalate your own efforts.

If you are going to another workplace to talk about your dispute and ask for support, you may at times find difficulty getting in – security guards may be suspicious and so on. Try to ring up the convenor beforehand and arrange for him to meet you; or, tell security to ring him as he is expecting you and then speak to him over the phone.

Remember: today blacking is probably the central weapon in most disputes. Effective blacking is the best way to minimize the hardship of the dispute to all by getting a quick solution. Many disputes have recently been lost because blacking was not effective.

Picketing   The more successful blacking is, the less you will need to depend on picketing. Some picketing is essential in any dispute but the less you are *dependent* on it the better off you are likely to be.
Workers picket:

● *To persuade workers not to go into work*   You should talk to those who are crossing the picket line. Do not simply abuse them. They may be misled or intimidated, at least initially. Try to explain patiently to them why what they are doing is wrong. Be polite and firm but do not be friendly. Take down their names and if after a few days it is clear persuasion will not work, point out the problems for them if you win the dispute.

You might be in the situation where you are an office worker involved in a dispute and shop-floor workers are crossing your lines. This may be because in the past, office workers have done the same to the manual union. Here you should go to the shop-stewards and argue that while there have been problems in the past you are now going forwards. If they fail to support you now they will be going *backwards*. If they take a stand then when the dispute is over you may be able to help them in future.

● *To persuade workers from services, customers and suppliers not to help the employer by making deliveries* You should stop all vehicles and explain to them what your dispute is about. Ask them to turn back and report to their own senior stewards what the situation is. Tell them you or the full-time official will be in touch. If a driver insists on crossing your picket line take down his details so that you can report him to the union. Similarly, with non-union drivers you can point out that you have taken their details and that you will contact union members at other places where they deliver, who will refuse to handle their goods. You should also try and ensure that postmen do not deliver. In certain cases, as at Grunwick, this can have a crippling effect on a firm's business. Once again: effective blacking removes many of these problems. The matter is simply dealt with at the other end, though there is still the need for vigilance as your employer can always hire substitute cowboy outfits.

In many cases, where official and formal approaches are not leading to blacking, workers use flying pickets in order to stop goods entering or leaving other workplaces. Flying pickets can be used when you have formally requested blacking, gone to speak to the stewards at the workplace involved but you are obviously not getting anywhere. A group of you may therefore have to picket this other workplace.

In recent years, where picketing with small groups of workers has not been effective, workers have taken part in mass pickets. Here, they have attempted to mobilize enough fellow workers to prevent workers or goods going in or out of the workplace. This tactic was seen at its most effective in the famous incident at Saltley Gates in the 1972 miners strike where a mass picket closed down the depot. A mass picket may have an immediate success. However, the Grunwick dispute showed that its success can be limited. In this case, the authorities simply brought in more and more police as the number of pickets grew, and showed themselves determined to break the picket lines at any costs. The Special Patrol Group too have been in evidence in picket lines in many recent disputes. A mass picket can be very useful for increasing morale and gaining publicity and showing solidarity. It is no substitute for effective blacking.

The strike committee

There may be a need to change the strike committee as new workers develop and as some members drop out. You should give each member a special responsibility. Here are some of the areas you will need to consider:

Picketing It is important that an effective rota should be drawn up involving all workers. Every picketing spell of duty should be covered by sufficient workers to ensure observance of the line. Make sure that picketing stewards are made responsible for each group of pickets and are well briefed by the committee member responsible. Contact should be made with the police so that you can try to ensure that they co-operate in allowing you to stop vehicles and workers to present your case. It is important to have discipline on the line at all times; the arrest of activists can have a weakening impact on a stoppage. Whilst offers of help on picket lines are welcome because they show a belief in union solidarity, you have to make sure that those directly involved are aware of the discipline of the picket line. In case you *do* have any problems make sure that you can quickly contact a solicitor and full-time official and that all workers are aware of their legal rights.

191

Finance It is important that your union makes the dispute official as soon as possible. This will not only ensure payment to the strikers but it will mean that it may be easier to convince other workers to black goods and respect picket lines. Your union will have a procedure for making strikes official. You should be aware of this and make sure that it is operating. If not, pressurize your full-time official and relevant union body. However, the sum of money you will receive in strike pay will be relatively small. Many union rulebooks provide for levies to be put on other workers so that they can help those in dispute. This generally has to be authorized at district or regional level. You should find out how the system operates from your rulebook or full-time official and set the wheels in motion.

You will also need to raise money by more informal means. What workers normally do is get a uniform appeal sheet printed. You should head the sheet with a brief statement of what your dispute involves, when it began, who is involved and why the dispute is relevant to other workers. You should then ask for donations and messages of support and give an address to which they can be sent. Stamp the sheet with a branch stamp. You can then circulate sheets to union branches, shop-steward's committees and trades councils.

You will need somebody with a head for figures, to administer cash on behalf of the strike committee. There should be a hardship fund for those with problems. It is not good for morale if individual strikers take temporary jobs, but if they do you should try and ensure that they pay a proportion of their earnings into this fund.

Social security Somebody should be responsible for helping all workers who are going to be claiming social security. As with the police it might be useful if you go to the social security office and explain the situation to the relevant official. You should also ask for the leaflets which give details as to what you can claim and how to claim it. (Leaflets SB1 and SB2.) Workers should always go in groups to claim and if the social security are being uncooperative, a sit-in in the office may be useful.

You may get useful help and advice from your local trades council; a claimants union; a law centre; or your union legal department.

Remember too that workers at the social security will be in a union, generally the CPSA, and if you have real difficulties you can get in touch with their branch to explain your problems and request cooperation.

Publicity You should be able to get reproduction and printing facilities from your local branch or trades council. On the picket line, visiting another workplace or attending a branch meeting, you should always take leaflets explaining your case and asking for help.

Trade unionists generally find that the stories which appear in the press about their dispute bear little resemblance to what is actually going on. Once again you may be able to get in touch with an NUJ Father of the Chapel and discuss the situation. If you are going to talk to the press, it is probably best to have one press officer who will deal with them rather than each worker giving individual versions which can only aid the distortion process.

Remember:

- Never neglect the involvement of *all* members in the strike. If you do then the strike committee may end up as the only workers left on strike! Hold regular meetings of all strikers and ensure that they are all kept busy. Boredom kills involvement.

- Two golden rules for occupations: strict security and no ale on the premises.

- Do not forget about entertainment, films and plays, and visiting speakers. This helps to keep up morale and participation.

- It is also *crucial* to involve husbands and wives of strikers. In most disputes, strikers' families give them loyalty and support. Examples blown up in the press of wives nagging husbands back to work happen in a minute number of cases. Nevertheless, it is useful to hold a meeting for all workers' families early on in a strike, so that the situation can be explained and discussed and wives and husbands will see that there are others in the same position as they are.

● Do not forget about your own union. Send representatives to meetings of all bodies – branches, district and regional councils so that you can be aware of what you should be getting from the union in terms of money, solidarity and support. If you are not getting what you are entitled to, use your democratic rights and push, push, push!

● Do not forget about the wider union movement. Organize speakers to publicize your case in *all* labour movement bodies. Trades councils are particularly important. Try and get the trades council to organize a demonstration in support of your dispute. It may also be useful to try and establish a support committee consisting of representatives of other union bodies to coordinate help for your dispute.

Industrial action and the law

As the factory system developed and employers started hiring workers, the judges and lawyers said that employers and workers were making a contract of employment. A contract is a legally enforceable agreement. If one side breaks it the other side can sue them for compensation. Moreover, if I induce John Smith who is a party to a contract with Bill Sykes to break it by making John a better offer, then Bill can sue John for breaking the contract *and* he can sue me for inducing John to break that contract. This seems to do rough justice between John and Bill. It does not work quite so well with trade unionists and employers. If a union official calls workers out on strike or instructs them to black certain kinds of work, then more often than not the workers will be breaking their contracts of employment and the official may be said to have induced them to do this. By inducing workers to break their contracts of employment the official could be said to be indirectly inducing a breach of the commercial contracts that the worker's employers had with customers and suppliers. Most industrial action would then be illegal. For example, a worker standing on a picket line who successfully asked a lorry driver to turn back might be said to be inducing that driver to break his contract of employment and by doing that he might be inducing a breach of the commercial contract between his boss and the lorry driver's boss. In all sorts of cases the bosses could get legal orders or injunctions saying that union action was illegal and should be called off.

In a full legal hearing the employer would have to prove that trade unionists knew about the contracts involved, that they intended to break them and other legal technicalities. They have been able to get over this by what is called an interim injunction. As the full trial may take months, the courts will be prepared to have a quick hearing and if the employer can show that on the face of it he has some sort of case, the court will generally decide that the status quo should be maintained until the full hearing – otherwise the employer would lose production in what may have turned out to be an illegal strike. This interim injunction procedure is based on the myth that workers lose nothing by this cooling off period. They can take action after the full case. In reality this meant that workers were negotiating with one hand tied behind their backs. They had to forget about what might be a pressing problem or, without the ability to take industrial action, accept a second best solution.

Trade unions ran campaigns to get protection from Parliament from this law made by judges which would mean that they could not operate effectively. Rather than giving unions a positive right to strike or picket, Parliament decided to simply give unions immunity from the general law. To argue that this minimal protection needed to allow unions to operate, gave unions privileges or put them above the law is nonsense.

Basically, the law did two things:

- It protected unions from actions for inducing breach of contract and committing other legal wrongs where they were acting in contemplation or furtherance of a trade dispute.
- It allowed workers to picket at or near any place of work in order to peacefully persuade people not to work where they were acting in contemplation or furtherance of a trade dispute.

A trade dispute covers most matters over which you would take industrial action – terms and conditions for employment, hiring or firing, discipline, membership of a union, or procedures for negotiation. The major area the judges have said are not covered are 'political disputes' – if, for example, you take action against government legislation or policies.

In recent years the courts undermined these protections given to trade unionists. They said that all kinds of legitimate blacking were not in furtherance of the initial trade dispute. They said pickets could attend at a workplace but they could not stop a lorry driver or a person on foot to argue their case. The numbers of pickets and what they could do was completely at the discretion of the police. If pickets did not follow police instructions then they could be prosecuted in a criminal court for offences such as obstructing the police, obstructing the highway or public nuisance.

The Employment Act, 1980, puts the top hat on the judges recent attempts to deprive workers of legal protections. When you are taking industrial action, you will only be legally protected against actions for breach of contract when you are picketing your own place of work. If you go off to picket another factory where there is a recognition dispute or you simply picket another hospital in your health authority then you will be open to legal action. A union official is protected if he is picketing with members whom he represents at their own place of work. If you work at more than one workplace you will be entitled to picket only the place from which you work or from where your work is administered. Sacked workers will be entitled to picket their former workplaces.

The Act also makes it very difficult for trade unionists to be legally protected when they are involved in blacking. You are only protected when you induce breaches of contract involving employers who are not directly parties to the dispute if your purpose or principal purpose was to directly disrupt the supply of goods and services to your employer and your action was likely to achieve that purpose. You will also be protected if you are taking action with these pre-conditions against an associated employer of your employer who is providing substitute goods for the ones that you are blacking. These sections of the Act give our biased judiciary the power to decide on the purpose and effectiveness of industrial action. In one case, for example, they decided that secondary action was taken not to bring pressure to bear on the employer but to raise the morale of the strikers – as if the two things could be separated. In another case where blacking of adverts meant that a newspaper was appearing with blank pages, the court held that the blacking was not achieving its purpose.

The basic attitude of trade unions to these provisions of the Employment Act should be: *business as usual*. Look at the points which we have made, decide what is the most effective way to organize your action, what is required to win the dispute and use those tactics.

Further reading

For some graphic accounts of strikes in the past, see R. Leeson, *Strike: a live history, 1887–1971* (Allen and Unwin, 1973). Most of the issues, problems and controversies which surround industrial action are discussed in R. Hyman, *Strikes* (Fontana, 1977). A more practical guide for shop-stewards is E. Johnston's *Industrial Action* (Arrow, 1976).

Conclusion

We would like to think that you will have agreed with many of the ideas and arguments put forward in this book. More important, however, is whether reading it has made you think about and question many of the second rate ideas and attitudes about trade unions which are accepted without a second thought and which unfortunately stop many workers playing any role in their organizations.

Becoming a trade union member or activist today is more challenging than at any time since 1945. Workers are being blamed for economic problems that they did nothing to create and are being asked to foot the bill in terms of a level of unemployment not seen since the 1930s, reductions in wages and cuts in the welfare state. For the first time in twenty years, trade unions are losing members. Many of the gains that have been made since the war are at risk. However, the trade union movement has still maintained its overall position. It has not been weakened in any decisive way. It is still the only factor that stands between the working class and a return to the conditions of the 1930s.

In these conditions the most important challenge is not simply to protect the day to day interests of trade union members, for we shall find even protection of interests impossible in the 1980s unless we look again at trade union purpose, organization and democracy to see how we can improve our organizations to better face the task of developing broader solutions to today's problems which will be in the interests of all workers. The way the trade union movement goes in the next decade will be a vital factor in the way society goes. The way the union and society develop depends on you and thousands of other members like you.

As in the past, the starting point still has to be the workplace. A movement which does not relate to the everyday concerns of ordinary workers and capture their interest and imagination will have no roots and will not grow. But if we are to succeed in protecting our interests here then we have to look upwards to the rest of our union and outwards towards other trade unions whose members in the end have interests which are the same as ours. More than that, we have to realize that collective bargaining with the employer, no matter how broad and sophisticated, and whilst it is an essential protection, is not enough.

If trade unionists leave control over economic decisions to politicians, civil servants and management in a society where production is based on profit then we may, after five or six lean years, have an upturn in the economy followed by yet another crisis. If we want a more guaranteed and civilized way of running society, then we need a new system which will directly involve the workers who produce the goods in taking economic decisions and planning production. The challenge facing trade unionists in the next decade is to push, through the Labour Party, for change at government level and also to develop detailed and concrete alternatives at plant, industry and national level to today's moribund economic system.

Government action is vital but is in itself insufficient. In the end, the future of workers is in their own hands. The words John Steinbeck wrote of the 1930s apply now: 'In the eyes of the people there is a failure and in the eyes of the hungry there is a growing wrath.' We must make sure that the solution does not slip through our fingers today as it did yesterday.

Select further reading

Some books are mentioned at the end of each chapter which will help you to go further with the particular subject discussed. In some we haven't done this because there aren't any. However, don't forget that the TUC and individual unions produce a wide range of pamphlets and handbooks on such issues as law, new technology, health and safety, pensions, the job of the shop-steward and how unions work. Make sure that you keep up to date with these.

If you want to deepen your understanding of trade unions, the following books are worth reading. Some may be a bit expensive, but you can borrow them from the public library.

There are four general books you will find useful:

H. A. Clegg, *The Changing System of Industrial Relations in Great Britain* (Blackwell)
K. Coates and T. Topham, *Trade Unions in Britain*, (Spokesman)
R. Hyman, *Industrial Relations – A Marxist Introduction* (Macmillan)
ACAS *Handbook of Industrial Relations* (HMSO)

If you want to look at the history of trade unions in more depth, E. P. Thompson's *The Making of the English Working Class* (Pelican, 1970) deals with the industrial revolution, J. Hinton's *The First Shop Stewards' Movement* (Allen and Unwin, 1973) looks at the origins of shop stewards, and a brief general account is H. Pelling, *A History of British Trade Unionism*, (Pelican).

The economic framework in which unions operate is analysed in: A. Glynn and J. Harrison, *The Great British Economic Disaster* (Pluto, 1980) an alternative explanation of some of the issues is G. Hodgson *Socialist Economic Strategy* (ILP).

The problems women have faced in trade unions are described in: S. Boston, *Women workers and the Trade Unions*

(Davis Poynter, 1980). There is nothing of practical use on race and trade unions and you will have to rely on leaflets and pamphlets from the Commission for Racial Equality and the Runnymede Trust.

On the relationship between the trade unions and the Labour Party see: R. Miliband, *Parliamentary Socialism*, (Merlin, 1972), D. Coates, *Labour and Power* (Longman, 1980) and L. Panitch, *Social Democracy and Industrial Militancy* (Cambridge, 1976).

On the law and union rights, J. McMullen, *Rights at Work* (Pluto, 1978) and P. O'Higgins, *Workers' Rights* (Arrow, 1976) give a detailed and practical analysis for the shop-steward. For the basic points of taking a tribunal case J. McIlroy, *Going to Law* (Sweet and Maxwell, 1980).

On health and safety, P. Kinnersly, *The Hazards of Work* (Pluto, 1972), is a practical handbook every trade unionist should read. The WEA series *Studies for Trade Unionists* contains several useful pamphlets on health and safety.

There is little that is useful on skills or industrial action. Apart from E. Johnston, *Industrial Action* (Arrow, 1976) there is nothing written from a union angle on running a strike or how to negotiate. If you want to start finding out about your employer, look at M. Barratt Brown, *Information at Work*, (Arrow, 1978) and C. Hird *Your Employer's Profits* (Pluto, 1975). If you want to go into very lengthy detail about meeting procedure, see W. Citrine, *The ABC of Chairmanship*, (NCLC Publishing Co. 1968).

Index